How to Buy a Home

Coming Soon:
(Also available in Spanish)

How to Fix Your Credit

There Is an Answer: How to Prevent and
Understand HIV/AIDS

How to Write a Resume and Get a Job

U.S. Citizenship for You and Your Family

How to Buy a Home

The Reverend Luis Cortés Jr.

ATRIA BOOKS

NEW YORK LONDON TORONTO SYDNEY

ATRIA BOOKS

1230 Avenue of the Americas
New York, NY 10020

Library of Congress Cataloging-in-Publication Data

Cortés, Luis, Rev.
    How to buy a home / Reverend Luis Cortés Jr.
       p.   cm.—(Esperanza series)
    Includes bibliographical references.
    ISBN-13: 978-0-7432-8790-6

    1. House buying—United States. 2. Home ownership—United States.
3. Home—United States—Religious aspects. I. Title. II. Series.

HD259.C665 2006
643'.120973—dc22   2005058895

First Atria Books trade paperback edition May 2006

10 9 8 7 6 5 4 3 2 1

For information regarding special discounts for bulk purchases,
please contact Simon & Schuster Special Sales at 1-800-456-6798
or business@simonandschuster.com.

Contents

Introduction

It is the dream of thousands of Americans. To own the house that they call their home, to be able to go to sleep knowing and feeling a sense of permanence in their lives. Your dream of owning a home can come true! It may take hard work. You must learn about buying and owning a house. You may have to change some spending habits. This book will help you along the way to understand the process of buying a house:

- It will help you think about why you want to own a house;
- It will help you know if you are ready to own a house;
- It will help you plan for buying a house;
- It will help you understand the basic steps of purchasing a house;
- It will help you learn about the people you will work with in buying a house;
- It will help you understand the language used by the banks and others who will work with you;
- It will give you the needed practice to fill out important forms;
- It will help you to keep your house once you buy it.

This book also contains samples of the documents you will need to complete and sign during the home-buying process; a list of important words you will hear, read, and use; and a list of other materials you can read to better understand the home-buying process. We will also provide you with a special code by which you can get more free information at our website.

Many people may tell you that buying a house is not possible; that owning a house is out of reach. But I have seen many who saw that turn around, and after years of saving they reached their homeownership goal. How! They learned the process, developed a plan, set a goal, and worked toward it. You, too, can try, and at each step in the process of buying a home, you can open this book again and again to keep learning.

One challenge of home ownership is a financial one. Another is turning your house into a home. This book will also touch on these subjects, and the good news is that if you have to defer your home-ownership goal because you need a long-term savings plan, you can still start making a home immediately. We will explore some of the ways we can use to make any place we find into a home for ourselves and our family. The American dream of house, family, and future can be yours! I pray that this book will be a way to whet your appetite for the process of buying a house and give the reasons why buying a house and turning it into a home will be a blessing to you and your loved ones.

I wish you success in reaching your dream of owning a home. With God's help and some hard work, you will be successful!

The Reverend Luis Cortés Jr.
How to Buy a Home

How to Buy a Home

1

Buying a House and Making a Home

Making a House into a Home

Anyone who hears and obeys these teachings of mine is like a wise person who built a house on solid rock. Rain poured down, rivers flooded, and winds beat against that house. But it did not fall, because it was built on solid rock. Anyone who hears my teachings and doesn't obey them is like a foolish person who built a house on sand. The rain poured down, the rivers flooded, and the winds blew and beat against that house. Finally, it fell with a crash.

MATTHEW 7:24–27 CEV

The above scripture is obvious to us: if we build upon a rock, a strong foundation, the house will survive hard times. The purchase of a house does not create a home; in fact, a home is not predicated by ownership of property but by a mind-set that creates the temperamental and environmental conditions, thereby creating a physical place that has deep spiritual significance. A home radiates security, love, nurture, and a connectedness among all who live in it and those who enter its doors. How then can we achieve the transformation of a house to a home? Why would we want to create it? How can we build a solid foundation for our family?

A house that becomes a home creates stability for your family. Those who own homes are more likely to better adapt to American aspirations and values.

A study by the U.S. Department of Housing and Urban Development put it this way:

> The desire for home ownership is deeply rooted in the American psyche. Owning a home embodies the promise of individual autonomy and of material and spiritual well-being that many people sought in coming to this country. In addition to its functional importance and economic value, home ownership has traditionally conveyed social status and political standing. It is even thought to promote thrift, stability, neighborliness, and other individual and civic virtues.

Home Ownership Creates Wealth

Purchasing a home is the largest investment that most families will ever make. It is in effect a forced savings plan in that part of your mortgage payments is retained as equity in your house. As long as the value of the home does not erode, there is a long-term wealth benefit. As a general trend, owning a home is a good long-term investment. Home ownership has become a critical factor in moving up the economic ladder as home equity is the largest single source of household wealth for most Americans. For homeowners, almost 60 percent of their wealth is in the form of home equity. For minority homeowners, home equity is an even more important component of wealth, representing more than three-fourths of their median net wealth. Homeowners also enjoy important tax advantages in the value and distribution of federal tax preferences for home ownership, such as the deductibility of property taxes and mortgage interest and the onetime exclusion of capital gains.

Home Ownership Creates Personal Well-being

Home ownership is a commonly recognized symbol of social status and an important goal for many Americans. It improves our self-esteem and life satisfaction. Owning a home is a widely shared and cherished goal and an expectation and hope of most Americans. Many scholars have reasoned that its attainment tends to increase the homeowner's contentment with life. It is often argued that home ownership enhances the homeowner's sense of control over his or her life and environment by offering greater privacy and protection. Empowerment comes from the ability to own, change, and control one's environment, to be able to paint, change fixtures, and change the inside or outside of your house. Your living space will better support your lifestyle and may increase your satisfaction with your house and life. To know that one will not have to negotiate new leases with their unpredictability is also a part of both financial and geographic control that promotes well being. Homeowners control who comes into their house. The social status and freedom of home ownership can lead to higher levels of self-esteem and a belief in the greater control over life in general.

Home Ownership Creates a Healthier Family

Psychologically we have already noted that the self-esteem of home-owners is higher than those who don't own their own homes. Studies attribute this to three underlying factors: first, the purchase of a home leads to others holding us in high regard; second, as homeowners we understand ourselves as doing better; and third, we see ourselves as successful in accomplishing goals, our purchase being evidence of our competence. The vast majority of home buyers have stated that being a homeowner makes them feel better about themselves. Employed homeowners report significantly less economic strain, depression, and problematic alcohol use than do renters. Home ownership contributes both to psychological health and physical health. Homeowners do not have to deal with landlords who provide inadequate heating and cooling, and they also suffer less of the infestation of bugs and rodents that can lead to respiratory and other illnesses. Homeowners also score higher on general health questionnaires and health indicators.

Home Ownership Creates a Better Educational Environment for Your Children

There seems to be no better reason for homeownership than what studies tell us regarding our children. Homeowners tend to create a higher quality home environment for children. Children are better supported in their physical, emotional, and learning development. Children will perform better in mathematics and reading tests; will be less likely to drop out of high school, to have children as teenagers, or to be arrested prior to age eighteen. In other words, children who live in their own homes tend to do better in school and are less likely to participate in behaviors that are detrimental to their future development. Children of homeowners tend to become homeowners themselves. Doing better in school and getting in less trouble leads to increased earnings and the acquisition of a home.

Home Ownership Creates More Stability in the Neighborhood

Family stability contributes to and is enhanced by the stability that home ownership provides to the neighborhood. We already noted that there will be less delinquency among the youth, and studies show that there is less addiction to alcohol or drugs by adults.One of the most persistent claims made for home ownership is that owners have a greater financial and emotional investment in their neighborhood and are more likely to maintain and improve their neighborhood. Homeowners have lower residential turnover as home buying is viewed as signifying a family's commitment to remain in the community. This commitment of home buyers also affects rental residents: they are also less likely to move away from the neighborhood. One of the reasons for this is that homeowners are more likely than absentee landlords or their renters to maintain and improve their properties. Homeowners spent more on maintenance, were less likely to defer repairs, and reported fewer housing problems. Home ownership creates a higher level of neighboring: the forming of neighborhood or block associations that lead to better understanding of political and local neighborhood leadership. Items of mutual interest, such as police, fire, and school needs, are shared by neighbors. Neighborhood community building leads to the development of crime prevention programs, such as a neighborhood watch. Even when cooperating to stop illegal activity, home-owning neighbors are more likely to look out for each other.

Now we have discovered many of the reasons we should strive to be a homeowner. Home ownership can help us create: wealth, personal well-being, a healthier family environment, better educational achievement by our children, and greater family and neighborhood stability. If you can afford to purchase a home you should consider it.

We started this chapter with a sacred scripture, a parable that forcefully illustrates a single idea. This story is about two persons, each building a house. One uses a rock as a foundation; the other uses sand. A wise person, we are told, builds on a secure foundation; a foolish person gives no thought to the foundation. The parable conveys to us that we have to prepare for hard times and that hard times will come to all of us. Rain, floods, and wind will come into our lives in many different forms and venues. Clearly, the parable shares with us the need for a strong foundation to face the storms of life. These storms can be inflicted by crime or accident or our very own actions, and they can sink our family, friends, or loved ones, attacking our health, finances, or relationships. To repel or withstand these unwanted events, it is important to have your home spiritually centered, which is what is meant by building on the rock, so that when the storm comes—and it will—you can withstand it and survive it. Building on a rock assists us in transforming a house into a home. Unlike a house that can be purchased, building on the rock necessitates developing an inner spirituality that becomes a part of your life and a part of how you deal with adversity. It is the security that God is present in your life and that God's love for you is unwavering. It is faith, an acceptance that God is both concerned for you and desirous of a relationship with you. This relationship can be instrumental in converting your house into a home. It can help center your entire family and those who enter your house as you express your love and care for them. It is an understanding that God is desirous of a relationship with you and that God is active in pursuing that relationship. God will help you become a woman or man of greater substance, living a life that will not crumble under pressure or sink in sand when the storm comes by. You can be a person who can face the storm and not have the house come down. It will be because you have chosen to connect to God. You have become strong on the inside. You have become someone who has learned to walk with God this day and the next day and the next. Facing whatever it is you have to face, the day that brings the storm will be no different from the ones that preceded it. God will be your companion then because you have made a practice of hearing and obeying God's voice, and your life will have a foundation under it. You will be able to deal with whatever tragedy life may bring. Building a strong foundation requires faith, which in fact is the foundation. The foundation grows stronger as you learn to believe that God listens and forgives and that God does so because God loves.

God Listens

Developing your spiritual center begins with the realization that God does indeed listen. While this seems simple, it truly is not. Many people feel that God can't possibly care about our inconsequential or insignificant selves, given all the people and needs in the world. Others cannot come to grips with the idea that God would listen to them, given the things they have done to and not done for themselves and others. For whatever the reason, many of us deeply believe we cannot approach God. If you talk to God, God will listen. All you need to do is try. What kind of prayer does God listen to? There are three things God wants us to do: first, we must pray from the heart; second, we must acknowledge our need and our pain, hiding nothing; third, we need faith. Prayer must be from the heart. It should be pure, meaning that there is nothing contrived about it, a conversation. It can be full of emotion as we cry to, call to, nag, whisper to, or remain silent before God. Our prayers are to acknowledge both God's existence and our needs. We cannot hide anything from God. He knows our innermost being. He knows our strengths and our weaknesses. How can we keep any of our needs from God? There are times we are unsure of God's guidance because of the pain we incur and the struggles we face. But as we persevere we can look back and see God guiding our life and that of our family and friends each step of the way. What do we really need? God knows our desires. God knows our needs better than we do ourselves. We make requests to God because he is merciful. In our prayer we should give adoration and acknowledge God as creator and sustainer. We confess our faults. We give thanks to God for our lives. We present to God our supplications and our needs. We may desire a house for the development of our family. For you to pray and ask for God's blessing in the process of acquiring a house is not only appropriate, it is the first step in making your future house into a home.

God Forgives

Forgiveness is an action of God that takes away the obstacles and barriers that separate humans from God's presence, opening the way to reconciliation and a relationship with God. God desires to have a healthy and whole relationship with every human being. Our insistence on disobedience, the straying from God's desires, cuts us off from this relationship. Forgiveness is the removal of the barriers between us and God. Understanding that forgiveness is a gift that God truly wants to bestow upon us is an important part of the foundation that creates a spiritually centered home. Forgiveness is the glue that will enable you to withstand the storms that hit your house. The forgiveness that God will bestow upon you should in turn be bestowed on others. In creating a home, members of a family will inevitably fail each other. Forgiveness will have to be taught and practiced for any family to survive. We should always remember that we are creatures who can never deserve the forgiveness that God Almighty bestows, yet we receive it because of God's love for us. God in turn asks us to bestow forgiveness on others.

God Loves

That God is about and for love is unquestionable. When Christ was asked, "What are the greatest commandments," he answered, "Love the Lord your God and love your neighbor as yourself," implying that God is both lovable and loving. It is this divine love that will go to any length to do good to humanity and secure our well-being. God's activity is to love, and God implores humanity to reciprocate by loving God and each other. As Christians, we understand that God's love is so strong that the writer of the Gospel of John states, "For God so loved the world that He gave his only begotten Son, that whoever believes in Him should not perish but have everlasting life" (John 3:16). What is amazing is that God loves us and that because of that love God will listen to us and forgive us. As you continue to reflect and meditate on God's love, you will connect with the presence of God; you will begin to grow in confidence that God listens, forgives, and loves. The process of connectedness can be assisted by your relationship to a house of worship, clergy, and others who are in search of God's love. This connection will eventually provoke you to find the opportunity to use your growing faith to serve others, starting with those who live with you and those who live near you or visit you. As you grow in understanding God's love for you, you will grow in your capacity to love others. As we hear of God's love we will learn to act on God's love. Loving others reflects the nature of God that is in us and is evidence that we are God's children. Our understanding of this and our acting on it by talking to God begins the construction of our home, whose foundation is on a rock, not on the sand. Now you can convert the physical place called your house to the spiritual center called home.

A Home

A famous American poet once wrote, "Home is the place where, when you have to go there, / They have to take you in." That remark has been used for close to one hundred years because it encapsulates something that is so true. We all hope to have a place like that, a place that serves as a refuge, where if we are weary we can rest, where if we are hungry we can eat, and where if we thirst we will be given drink. This is the type of environment you want to create for your family. Before you find and purchase your house, prepare yourself and your family by developing the financial and spiritual foundations for your home we have discussed in this book. As soon as you move into your house, you begin its physical conversion. You create special places that promote family history, tradition, and culture, be they photos of special moments from the past and present; books that were important to you or to other family members that you want your children to read; ceramics, pictures, paintings, carpets; anything that has a family story attached to it that should be shared and passed along to others. These physical things will be bound together by love. These spaces are created not by the investment of money but by the investment of time. Simple actions are those that are most remembered. The glass of milk and plate of cookies for your children as soon as you see them when you get home from work and your telling them, "Don't let this spoil your dinner"; the Saturday or Sunday cup of coffee with your spouse while you dream of the future. These small traditions, if done in love, become the things that help inspire and maintain a home, even through stormy times. Each space of the house can take on a special significance. Kitchen and dining rooms are excellent spaces where one can take a moment to share something good or something bad that has happened. Dreams can be shared there; hopes for the future and assistance for the struggles of the present day.

There should be no part of the house where parents and their children cannot play. Play is the most underrated aspect of the development of a spiritual center in the home. *Play with your children!* Play with them in their bedroom, in the living room, kitchen—anywhere you can see and create a smile for them and, as a consequence, for you. Watch television together. I know most people say not to watch TV, but I believe you should watch it with your children and spouse. As the children and you grow older, they will actually watch it with you. The programs you watched together become memories that bind you together spiritually. For children, their bedroom or yours can be a great place to share. The hustle and bustle of our days sometimes doesn't allow for all the family interaction we hope for. There is one time, though, that is a must for all children, and that is bedtime. *Read* to them before they go to sleep. *Pray* with them. Have them pray for others. Nothing you do will help them and the spiritual growth of your family more than this repetitive daily action. It will help the children understand intuitively that *a home is more than a house.* It will help them establish their spiritual center and contribute to the development of the home's spiritual center. It will help them grow into a home, and it will help you in the same way. As you create a home, you will find that many children, neighbors, and friends will want to be around you. They will want to share and be in the place they know is built on a rock. Share your home but protect it. It is something that is fragile. Remember that storms will always come. Do not allow others to bring their storms into your house. Always be hospitable but also be protective of the home that God has given you.

So now . . . let's go buy a house . . . and create that home that will have you dwell in God's favor . . . FOREVER!

2

Am I Ready to Buy and Own a House?

Are you ready to buy a house? Are you ready for the responsibility of owning a house? A major difference between renting and owning a house is that when you own your house there is no landlord to call. Whether to do repairs, upgrades, and cosmetic changes is entirely your decision. You decide what is to happen in your house. You must be able to manage your money and make wise decisions about investing money in your house. You must be ready to be a disciplined decision maker, both in preparing to buy a house and in keeping one. It is very important to take the time to determine if you are *ready to buy and own a house.* To do that, ask yourself these basic questions. The answers may tell you that you need more time to save money, learn how to purchase a house, or decide what neighborhood to move to.

- Do I know my monthly expenses?
- Will I qualify for a mortgage?
- Do I know the costs of buying and owning a house?
- What kind of house do I need? What kind of house do I want?
- Where do I want to live?
- Do I know the process of buying a house?

These questions are related to each other, and your capacity to answer them will revolve around your *employment, savings,* and *credit.* You will need to review all of these variables and their relationships to each

11

other to determine your readiness to purchase a house. In this section of the book, you will consider each question in detail. Once you have answered these questions for yourself, you will be ready to work with the professionals who can help you through the process of buying a house.

You should also understand the barriers to buying a house. While there are many, the major ones usually are:

❑ *Lack of information.* Most often, people who would like to own their own house do not have good information about the house-buying process. Lack of information keeps many qualified families, particularly those of lower income or those of ethnic minorities, from becoming homeowners or obtaining the lowest-cost financing available to them.

❑ *Rising home prices.* High prices force first-time home buyers to come up with more cash, take out larger loans, or settle for a lower-quality house than they would have chosen otherwise.

❑ *Lack of an employment history.* Not having a steady job, having a series of low-paying jobs, or suffering through a period of unemployment.

❑ *Lack of savings.* Many people who want to purchase a house have not saved enough money to start the process of becoming a homeowner.

❑ *High consumer debt.* Some people have not managed their credit spending well. They have too much debt and cannot afford another purchase.

❑ *Credit issues.* Some people are not ready to purchase a house because they have credit problems, such as no credit record, inaccurate credit information, or poor credit history.

This book will help you understand how to overcome the barriers to buying and owning a house, but before you begin, there are a few things you must remember if you want to get off to a successful start.

❑ Read the entire book. Don't get so excited that you stop halfway through the book or skip some parts altogether. Buying a house is going to be one of the most expensive purchases you will make. To have more information, or to review what you already know, is better than not having some information.

❑ Do not be frustrated by something you may not understand. *There is more help!* As the owner of this book you will have access to a special part of a website that will provide additional information, graphs, charts, and more detailed explanations of some items in this book. You can view them on your computer along with other important information, or you can download them as Miscosoft Word or Adobe files. There are also pages that help you clearly understand the mathematical computations by allowing you to interact with them.

There is even more help! If after seeing our website you need more help, send us a message and we will try to get you more assistance.

You are on the way to a great beginning, to a journey that will help you become a homeowner. Now let's get started in getting that house!

Do I Know My Monthly Expenses?

To buy a house, you need savings, a steady *income*, a good *credit* record, and a history of *employment*. We will discuss each of these separately. Most important, before you begin to try to buy a house, you will need to know your monthly income and your monthly expenses. This way you will know how much you can spend on a house or how you need to change your current spending. It is very important to spend only what you can afford on a home.

❑ *Know your monthly income.* How much money does your household earn each month? First you must know your *net income* and your *gross income*. The amount of your annual salary is your *gross annual income*. When you divide the amount of your salary by 12, you know your *gross monthly income*. Your net income is what is left after taxes, social security, and other deductions. If your spouse works, make sure you know his or her gross and net income, too.

❑ *Know your monthly expenses.* What does it cost to run your house-hold? These are your expenses. How much must you spend on rent and utilities? What does it cost to buy food and household supplies? How much does your family spend on commuting to work and school? How much do you spend on child care? How much money do you need for clothing and uniforms? How much do you spend on health insurance, medicine, and health care? Do you have monthly car payments? Do you have car insurance payments? Do you have other financial responsibilities, such as debts or paying for the care of an older parent or relatives?

Some bills come every few months, others once or twice a year. Don't forget to count these, too. If you pay a certain bill once a year, divide that number by 12 so you know how much money you need to keep aside for it. If bills come a few times a year, add up the total amount of dollars and divide it by 12; this is your monthly expenditure.

Start by keeping a record of all the money your family spends over a few months. Soon you will understand your financial responsibilities. You will also see where your family can manage money more carefully by cutting or changing certain costs.

Use this Household Expense Worksheet to list and track your monthly expenses. This worksheet is also found in chapter 8. It is also available for download at www.esperanza.us. Just click on the book cover and you will be able to download and print as many as you need. You will also find an interactive version of many of the documents that you will need. These interactive pages will do many of the mathematical computations for you.

Household Expense Worksheet

Instructions: Fill in your estimated monthly expenses in the second column.

Monthly Expenses	Monthly Payment
HOUSING	
Rent	
First mortgage	
Second mortgage	
Association dues	
Property taxes	
Lot rent	
Home maintenance	
AUTOMOBILE	
Gasoline	
Maintenance (oil / lubrication / tires)	
Auto tags / inspection	
FOOD	
Groceries	
Meals out	
School lunches	
Food / snacks at work	
UTILITIES	
Electric / gas / oil / propane	
Water / sewer / garbage	
Telephone / cell phone / beeper	
Cable TV / internet	

(Continued on following page)

Household Expense Worksheet (continued)

Monthly Expenses	Monthly Payment
INSURANCE	
Automobile	
Medical	
Life	
Renters / homeowners	
HEALTH CARE	
Drugs / medication	
Office visits / deductible	
Dental	
Optical	
CHILD CARE	
Day care / babysitter	
Allowances / kids' stuff	
Diapers / formula / baby supplies	
Child support	
INSTALLMENTS	
Car payments	
Student loans	
Tax installments (state, federal)	
Other	
CHARITABLE DONATIONS	
Church, charities	
EDUCATION	
School tuition and supplies	

(Continued on following page)

Household Expense Worksheet (continued)

Monthly Expenses	Monthly Payment
LEISURE	
Books / newspapers / magazines	
Movies / sporting events / entertainment	
Gifts / parties / holidays / cards	
Vacations / travel	
Alcohol	
Cigarettes / tobacco	
Hobbies / clubs	
Lottery / casinos / bingo	
MISCELLANEOUS	
Work tools and clothes / occupational dues	
Dry cleaning / laundry	
Home cleaning supplies	
Bus fares / ride shares / parking	
Personal care (shampoo / toothpaste, etc.)	
Bank service charges / postage	
Pet care / vet / food / medications	
Lawn / pool maintenance / home security	
Savings / reserve	
SUBTOTAL	
OTHER DEBT SERVICE	
PAST DUE PAYMENTS AND CHARGES	
TOTAL EXPENSES	

Will I Qualify for a Mortgage?

A *mortgage* is a loan from a bank or mortgage company that is used to buy a house. You repay the loan over time. You also pay the lender a percentage of the loan, called *interest,* for the use of the money.

By providing you with a mortgage, a bank or mortgage company is investing in you, so first you must show that you are a good investment. You will need to show the bank or mortgage company that you can be trusted and that you have the capacity to repay the loan. You must prove to the lender that you have a reliable source of income and that you have saved enough money to make part of the purchase yourself (the down payment) and to make the mortgage payment each month. The bank or mortgage company will also need to know about any debts you have and any money you owed and repaid in the past, whether you have made all the payments on time, and how much money you have saved.

Take the time to look at your household the way the bank or mortgage company will. Are you a good investment?

❏ Do you have a steady income?
❏ How much do you spend each month to pay off your debt? When will you pay off the debt? Do you have a plan for paying off the debt?
❏ Do you set money aside? These are your savings. Do you save money for emergencies and important purchases? Do you have other savings? For example, do you save money for retirement or college?

Know Your Credit History

Can you demonstrate to a lender that you can repay your mortgage? Do you have a good record of meeting your financial responsibilities? You can get an idea of your credit history by making three lists.

First, make a list of the debts you have paid off and the debts you have right now. This list should include car loans, other loans of any kind, and credit card debt.

Next, think about your other financial obligations, now or in the past: rent, utilities, phone. Make a list of these responsibilities. Even if you paid rent to a parent or other family member, put it on the list.

Finally, on another list, write down any bills or debts that you have had problems paying, now or in the past. The lenders will want to see this list. If there are too many items in the first or third list (debts now and problems past and present), you may have difficulty getting a loan. No matter where you begin, you can repair any problems so you can move closer to buying a house.

Know Your Employment History

Can you show that you have had steady employment for at least two years? If you have held your present job for less than two years, make a list of the jobs you have held. Start with the job you have now and end with the first job you held. Write down the dates you started and ended the job and the salary you earned.

Do I Understand the Costs of Buying and Owning a House?

Now it is time to think about the costs of buying and owning a house. In this section, you will learn how to estimate the amount you can afford to pay for a house and the costs of buying and owning a house. Most important, you will learn about buying what you can afford.

Lenders take risks when they lend money. For this reason, they want to be sure that your house payments are within your means. In other words, they want to make sure that you can afford to make your payments.

Therefore, lenders set limits. They limit the amount that borrowers can have in monthly debt payments. These limits are called the *housing ratio* (also called the front-end ratio), and the *debt-to-income ratio* (also called the back-end ratio). Don't worry about the specifics of these ratios right now. For now, all you need to understand is that mortgage loans are based on these ratios and that for every type of loan different percentages are used to calculate how much of a loan you can afford. Keep in mind that high debt will reduce the number of dollars you will have to pay off a loan. The more monthly debt payments you have, the smaller the amount you can spend for your house purchase.

A general standard for calculating a mortgage debt is the housing ratio. The housing ratio is generally 28 percent of your income; occasionally it is allowed to be higher. Let's take the traditional 28 percent of your income and try calculating your maximum allowable housing expense. This is the amount that puts you at the least risk of spending more than you can afford on a mortgage and is the first number that a banker or real estate agent would look at for mortgage affordability. Remember that a working model of this equation can be found at www.esperanza.us at no charge to you.

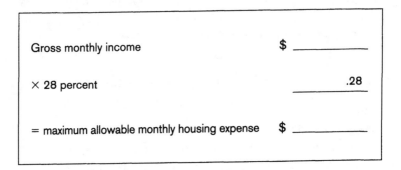

Gross monthly income $ _____

× 28 percent   _____ .28

= maximum allowable monthly housing expense $ _____

Buying the House

You will have to make a *down payment* on the house. You need to make most of this payment *from your own funds.* Cash gifts from others can be part of the down payment, but you will need to show where the funds came from. The down payment is not part of the mortgage loan. This payment is a portion of the total *sale* price of the house. The mortgage company or bank lends you the money for the remaining amount. The bigger the down payment you can make, the smaller the loan you will need. A smaller loan means lower monthly payments.

The amount of the down payment depends on many factors, such as any programs you may qualify for. But you should expect to pay from *2.5 to 20 percent* of the price of the house. There are rare exceptions to this; you may be able get a zero percent (0 percent) down payment mortgage.

When you purchase the house and make the settlement, you will need to pay certain costs, called *closing costs.* These are in addition to the price of the house. How much you will pay in closing costs will vary depending on where you live. A housing counselor, loan officer, realtor, bank, or mortgage company will tell you what closing costs to expect. (Later, we will explain who these people are and how they will help you buy a house.) You should ask your housing counselor if there are special programs available to help you with the closing costs.

Owning the House

Once you have made the down payment and paid the closing costs, you will make monthly payments on the mortgage loan. When you make a mortgage payment, part of it goes toward the *principal* (the amount of the loan) and part of it is *interest* (the money the lender charges for the loan). You must not miss any mortgage payments.

As you may know, the cost of your house is more than the monthly mortgage payment. You must also pay *local real estate taxes* and *homeowner's insurance.* These costs are sometimes included in your monthly mortgage payment, and the lender is responsible for seeing that the taxes and insurance are paid. If taxes and insurance are not part of the mortgage payment, you must plan and save to pay them when they are due. Also, the amount you pay for taxes and insurance will change over time. The lender may also require you to have *private mortgage insurance* (PMI). Private mortgage insurance is extra insurance that mortgage lenders require from most home buyers who obtain loans that are more than 80 percent of their new home's value. In other words, buyers with less than a 20 percent down payment are normally required to pay PMI.

BENEFITS OF PMI PMI plays an important role in the mortgage industry by protecting a lender against loss if a borrower defaults on a loan and by enabling borrowers with less cash to have greater access to home ownership. With this type of insurance, it is possible for you to buy a home with as little as 3 to 5 percent down payment. This means that you can buy a home sooner without waiting years to accumulate a large down payment.

For home mortgages signed *on or after* July 29, 1999, your PMI must—with certain exceptions—be terminated automatically when you reach 22 percent equity in your home, based on the original property value, if your mortgage payments are current. Your PMI can also be cancelled at your request—with certain exceptions—when you reach 20 percent equity in your home, based on the original property value, if your mortgage payments are current.

One exception is if your loan is "high-risk." Another is if you have not been current on your payments within the year prior to the time for termination or cancellation. A third is if you have other liens on your property. For these loans, your PMI may continue. Ask your lender or mortgage servicer (a company that collects your payments) for more information about these requirements.

On a $100,000 loan with 10 percent down ($10,000), PMI might cost you $40 a month. If you can cancel the PMI, you can save $480 a year and many thousands of dollars over the term of the loan. Check your annual escrow account statement or call your lender to find out exactly how much PMI is costing you each year.

When you own your house, you have freedom, stability, and security, but you also have responsibilities. You pay for utilities, repairs, and maintenance. Even if you and your family have the skills to make repairs and do the maintenance work, you will need to pay for materials. You may need to purchase appliances (refrigerator, stove, furnace, water heater, washer, and dryer) or replace them over time.

In your first year of owning a house, you will spend at least *$200 to $2,000* or more on materials, services, and improvements. After the first year, you can expect to spend *1 to 3 percent of the cost of the house* every year to maintain it.

You should save from 2 to 5 percent of your monthly income for maintenance and emergency repairs.

Know What You Can Afford

Start the process of buying a house by being very clear about the amount you can afford for a monthly mortgage payment. If you keep this amount in mind as you look at houses and speak with lenders, you will avoid committing yourself to a debt larger than you can afford to pay. You will buy within your means. By buying within your means, you will be sure to have enough money to meet all of your financial responsibilities, make your monthly mortgage payment, and maintain your home.

What Kind of House Do I Need and Want?

There are many types of houses. Look at the list of house types and think about what kind meets your needs.

KINDS OF STRUCTURES A house can come in many forms. It may be old, or it may be built to your specifications; it may be small or large, tall or low. It may be separate from other dwellings or attached to them. Here are some common structures.

Single A single house is separate from others and is on its own tract of land. Single homes come in many styles and sizes and may be either old or new. Single homes require maintenance of all exterior walls and the roof. The land around the house may be as small as a little yard in front and back or as large as several acres.

For example, a *ranch* home is a style of single house on one level. A ranch house may have a full or partial basement. Generally, a garage is attached to the side of the house. The major advantage is step-saving convenience.

A *mobile home* is also a single home. These one-floor houses are usually built on a steel chassis with wheels; the house is hauled to a

Single (two stories)

Single (ranch)

leased or owned site. The homeowner may make improvements and additions. When two houses are fastened along their length, it is called a double-wide. Limited in size, mobile homes are less expensive.

Twin (or semidetached) This house shares a side wall with another

Mobile home

house; usually the two houses are mirror opposites. Twins, or semidetached houses, are usually older. Twins may be priced lower than sin-
gles, and owners may see some savings in utility and maintenance costs.

Townhouse (or row house) Several houses are built together and

Twin (or semidetached)

connected by common or abutting walls. Townhouses may be old or new, ranging from the first houses built in the first cities in the United States to the houses currently being built in the suburbs. These houses are economical to maintain because they have small amounts of land around them and fewer exposed walls.

Multiunit (or multifamily) Structures (or single homes) are built or converted to contain two or more units. For example:

• *Duplex.* A single structure that contains two housing units.

Townhouse

Multiunit

Duplex

Triplex

- *Triplex.* A single structure that contains three housing units.
- *Fourplex.* A single structure that contains four housing units.

Some owners will purchase the entire structure, live in one unit, and rent out the others to cover the cost of the mortgage and for added income.

OTHER WAYS OF OWNING A HOUSE The terms condominium and cooperative refer to the arrangement for owning the house, not a specific structure.

Fourplex

Condominium (condo) Individuals purchase and own units of housing in a multiunit complex. The owners share financial responsibility (usually a monthly fee, called carrying charges) for maintenance of common areas and amenities. The owners association has regulations about maintenance and improvements to the units. Condominium complexes can range from apartmentlike units to townhouses and even single homes.

Cooperative (co-op) Residents purchase shares in a cooperative corporation that owns a multiunit building or complex; each shareholder is entitled to live in a specific unit and is responsible for paying a maintenance fee, which helps pay the expenses of running the building, including mortgage payments and real estate taxes. Like condominiums, co-op complexes can range from apartmentlike units to townhouses and even single homes.

Know What Kind of House You Need and Can Maintain

Decide what kind of house you need and can maintain by asking these questions:

❏ How many family members will live in your house? What kind of space will they need?

❑ What kind of exterior space and outbuildings do you need? (Do you need space for a business, vegetable garden, or livestock, for example?)

❑ Can you do the work of maintaining the exterior of the house and the property around it? Do you have the time, energy, and skills?

You must also decide how much work you can do, or want to do, to make the house livable. Do you want to be able to move right in? Are you willing to buy a house that needs some repairs? Do you have the time and the skills to renovate a house that needs a lot of work? Do you know enough about buildings and materials to supervise carpenters, plumbers, painters, and roofers?

A house that is in good condition will most likely cost more than one that needs repair. A house that needs a lot of work—renovation—may be a real bargain for someone who knows how to do the work (and has the time to do it) or can supervise a renovation project.

Do you want to buy an older house or a newer one? A new house will probably have a more modern design and layout and might be more energy-efficient and easier to maintain. The taxes may be higher, and it may be farther away from places you need to go to often. An older house may be in a more established neighborhood, closer to public transportation, and property taxes may be lower. But an older house often requires repairs and maintenance.

Building a house could be an option for you, especially if you live in an area of the country that has inexpensive land in either rural or urban areas. You can purchase plans and work with a reputable builder to create a house that meets your needs. There are also prefab kits and modular homes for low-income and middle-income owners. For information on the Rural Housing Services loans to build homes see chapter 4. There is also more information on building a house. See chapter 5.

Think about what kind of house is right for you and your family. Use the following list to decide what features the house must have. Make another list of the features you would like it to have. You will use these lists when you start to look at houses. The following Home-Buying Checklist is available at www.esperanza.us and is also included in chapter 8.

Home-Buying Checklist

1. What part of the town (or country) do you want to live in?

    _____

2. What price range can you afford?

3. Do you need to consider schools? Yes _____ No _____
    Specific needs: _____

4. Do you want a new home (less than five years old) or an older
    home? _____

5. What kind of houses are you willing to consider?
    Single____ Twin____ Duplex____ Triplex____ Fourplex____
    Mobile____ One floor____ Two or more floors____

6. What kind of buying arrangement are you willing to consider?
    Condo____ Co-op____ Lease-purchase____

7. How much renovation are you willing and able to do?
    A little____ A lot____ None____

8. Do you need to be close to public transportation?_____

9. Do you have any special access needs?_____

10. What do you need or want in a property?

	NEED	WOULD LIKE
Large lot (one-half acre or more)	_____	_____
Small lot (less than one-half acre)	_____	_____
Fenced yard	_____	_____
Garage	_____	_____
Carport	_____	_____
Patio/deck	_____	_____
Other buildings	_____	_____

11. How many bedrooms must you have?_____

12. How many bathrooms do you want?_____

13. How big a house do you need (square feet)?_____

14. What special features do you need (for example, an in-law apart-
    ment, storage, or facilities for animals)?_____

    _____

Where Do I Want to Live?

Deciding where you want to live is very important. You must think about the quality of your life and the soundness of your investment. Think about access to work, school, day care, and health care. You also need to think about the available houses in the community.

These questions will help you think about *where* you will buy a house:

❑ Does your family need access to public transportation? Do you need to be close to schools, shopping, and church? Do you need to be able to go to these places by walking or public transportation?

❑ How will you and your family members get to work? Is the neighborhood very far from work? How much time will you spend going to and from work?

❑ Is it important that your family is near a hospital or clinic? How will you get there from your house?

❑ What neighborhood or community seems right for you and your family? Would you feel welcome? Do the people in the community seem to share your values and interests? Are there places where your children or other family members can participate in activities that are important to them? Do you have family or friends in the neighborhood?

❑ Do you want to help build an emerging neighborhood? A type of house not affordable in one neighborhood or community may be affordable in a different one.

Make a list of what you need and want in a community.

3

How Do I Begin the Process of Buying a House?

Take the time to prepare to buy a house. Learn about the home-buying process and know what to expect.

Know the Process

Know what you must do to buy a house. Know the steps to home ownership:

- Learn the home-buying process;
- Know the professionals who can help every step of the way;
- Manage your money;
- Repair and establish credit;
- Know how much you can afford to spend on a house;
- Learn about mortgages;
- Avoid predatory lending;
- Get preapproved for a mortgage;
- Get a loan;
- Find a real estate agent and shop for a house;
- Enter a sales agreement;
- Make the settlement;
- Prepare a new budget and stick to it;
- Maintain your house.

This book explains each step of buying a house. It also describes the professionals who will help you in the process. Look for boxes labeled "Your Home-Buying Team" as you read this book. They will explain who these people are and how as part of your home-buying team they will work together to make your dream come true.

Learn the Home-Buying Process

We start by learning what the process is. You have already begun by purchasing this book. Don't allow strange words or an unknown experience to stop you from reaching your dream. Buying a house is like buying anything else: you have to know what you want, what you need, and what you can afford. In a way it is similar to buying a car: there is what we want and there is what we can afford. And as in buying a car, there can be traps to be avoided. Unlike buying a car, we can and do have a team of professional people to help you. You can learn to "kick the tires" and protect yourself in the purchase of a house.

❏ Read this book. Then, as you start each step of buying a house, reread the section of the book that describes that step.
❏ Seek assistance from a *certified housing counselor*. A housing counselor is someone with special training in the home-buying process. A certified housing counselor prepares you for homeownership by providing the education that will help you understand the responsibilities of purchasing and owning a home. Certified housing counselors offer *home-buyer education classes* in your community. You can find these classes by contacting your local city or township office or by contacting the office of Housing and Urban Development (HUD). Call 1-800-569-4287 or go to www.hud.gov. A housing counselor, sometimes called a mortgage counselor, can be of tremendous help. If you have a low or moderate income, their services may even be free. They can guide you through every step of this home-buying process. Try to find one as soon as you are sure that you are going to purchase a house. HUD also provides a twenty-four-page document

called "100 Questions & Answers about Buying a New Home" at
www.hud.gov/offices/hsg/sfh/buying/buyhm.cfm.

❏ In addition to working with a housing counselor, go to your *local
library* and ask the librarian to help you find books and other materials about the process of purchasing a house.

❏ Develop the habit of reading about real estate in your *local newspaper*. You can learn about prices for houses in the community where
you want to buy a house. You can also find current information on
mortgages in your region. This information will help you set your
financial goals.

Let's learn about the documents, the finances, and the people that are
part of the house-buying process. After reading this section of the
book, you will be ready to:

• Learn about your home-buying team;
• Start to learn about mortgages;
• Set goals and manage your money;
• Know your credit history;
• Maintain employment;
• Start collecting the financial documents you will need to apply for
a loan.

Know the Professionals Who Can Help You Get Started

Two professionals are very important in the early stages of the house-
buying process: a *certified housing counselor* and a *licensed real estate
agent*.

Set Goals and Manage Your Money

If you are serious about buying a house, you must manage your
money carefully.

Your Home-Buying Team

A *certified housing counselor* (also may be called a housing adviser or mortgage counselor) provides *free* education and advice about buying and maintaining a home. He or she can:

- Explain the process of buying a home;
- Explain your rights and responsibilities as a buyer;
- Help you determine the amount of mortgage you can afford, based on your income and debt;
- Give advice about sales agreements and loan documents;
- Assist in establishing credit or resolving credit problems;
- Help you avoid predatory lenders;
- Advise and assist you during the process, from finding a mortgage to the home inspection;
- Tell you about special programs you may qualify for;
- Explain how to manage your home and finances after your purchase.

Where to find a certified housing counselor

To find a certified housing counselor in your area, contact the office of Housing and Urban Development (HUD) by calling 1-800-569-4287 or going to www.hud.gov.

Licensed real estate agent

Choosing a *licensed real estate agent* is very important. This person should be someone you trust and respect as a knowledgeable professional. A real estate agent:

- Researches the available homes in your price range;
- Takes you to look at homes;
- Provides detailed information about each property: type, size, taxes;
- Helps you prepare a purchase offer;
- Deals with the paperwork to complete the sale.

You will learn more about real estate agents in chapter 5 of this book.

Begin Saving

Start to put money aside for a down payment and closing costs. Set an amount as a goal and figure out how long it will take you to reach it.

One way to save money is to pay yourself first. Try to set aside at least 5 to 10 percent of your take-home pay each paycheck. There are many ways to save money and to have that money earn still more money. Consider one, some, or all these accounts:

Regular savings account. An account maintained by a customer with a bank. A regular savings account is an interest-bearing one that's perfect for individuals or families. Its flexibility and convenience make it a great place to store a portion of your funds.

Club account. A savings account dedicated to a specific goal, such as holiday shopping or paying for a vacation, with weekly or biweekly deposits of a fixed amount.

Certificate of deposit (CD). An interest-earning savings account issued by a bank in which funds must remain on deposit for a specified time; withdrawals before maturity incur interest penalties. CDs usually offer a higher interest rate than most comparable investments. Also called a *time deposit.*

Money market account. A savings account offered by banks that pays a varying rate of interest as long as the balance does not fall below a predetermined minimum.

Matched savings account. An example is an IDA (individual development account). In a matched account, another organization, such as a foundation, corporation, or government entity, agrees to add a specific match of the money you deposited to your account.

Everyone in your household can contribute to the savings. Set family goals so all can help save and participate in the buying of the house.

Create a Spending Plan and Stick to It

It is important to control day-to-day spending. The way to control day-to-day spending is with a *budget*. A budget is a plan for how you will spend your money. Create a budget by writing down everything you spend money on. Then look carefully at the list. What can you cut out? Make sure that you and your family understand the difference between wants (what you would like to have or do) and needs (what you must have or do). Trim expenses down to the needs. Keep wants to a minimum.

Next, keep track of your family's spending. Record all purchases and bills. Are you sticking to the plan? Was it realistic? Can you cut more expenses? Can you augment your income? For example:

- Consider holding a yard sale.
- Consider selling a car.
- Check the interest rates on credit cards and perhaps negotiate a lower rate.
- Consider possible part-time or seasonal employment.

You can also trim your expenses. Here are a few suggestions:

- ❏ Buy only what you need.
- ❏ Make a list before you go shopping for food and other items and stick to it.
- ❏ Use coupons (but don't buy an item only because you have a coupon).
- ❏ Always try to pay cash. Do not use credit cards. If you use credit cards, pay them off immediately, avoiding interest and other charges.
- ❏ Avoid ATM fees. Withdraw cash at your ATMs, not elsewhere. Find other free or cooperating ATMs to avoid having to pay fees for getting to your own money. Do not use your ATM card for purchases if there are fees attached to your card's use. ATM fees can be very high for the amount of money that is usually transacted.
- ❏ Eat at home. Take your lunch (or breakfast or dinner) to work.

❑ Learn to make simple, nutritious meals with fresh ingredients instead of buying prepared foods at the market.

❑ Look for sales and off-season bargains on the items you need. Compare prices. Look for the items you need at discount stores, thrift stores, and flea markets.

❑ Use public transportation or share rides.

❑ Buy a used car instead of a new one with high monthly payments (but make sure the used car is in good condition so you do not spend money on expensive repairs).

❑ Stop or avoid all extra services, like cable TV. Use a cell phone or pager only if you need it for work or in an emergency.

❑ Avoid check-cashing stores, pawn shops, and rent-to-own stores. They charge fees and high interest. Start a checking account. Deposit your paycheck in the account and use your checks instead of money orders to pay bills.

Pay All Your Bills on Time

Your good habit of controlling spending is very important. You must also make sure that a lender knows you will repay your loan promptly. Your good habit of paying bills on time will help you assure the lender that you are a good risk for a mortgage.

You can avoid late payments by taking these steps:

❑ Know when bills are due. Think about when you must mail your payments so they arrive on or ahead of time. Mark on a calendar the day to mail your bill payments.

❑ Arrange to have bills paid automatically from your checking account each month. Utility and insurance companies make it possible for customers to do this. But be sure to subtract the automatic payments from the balance of your checking account.

❑ If you must be away when bills are due, make a plan for paying them on time. Prepare the bills and ask a family member or friend to mail them on a certain date. Call your creditors and arrange to pay bills ahead of time.

Keep Your Goal of Owning a House in Front of You

Meet as a family to talk about your progress toward your goal. Find a picture of the kind of house you want and display it in a place that everyone in the family sees often. Think about that picture before you shop or when you see something that you would like to buy but do not need.

Know Your Credit History

Make sure that the bank or mortgage company will want to invest in you. The lender wants to know about your *credit history*. Are you able to pay off the loan? The lender will want to know what debts you have had in the past and if you repaid them on time.

Establish a Credit History

If you have never had any debt (or debt in your name), you will not have a credit history. The lender will not be able to review a *credit report* to see if you are a good risk. You will have to establish credit if:

❏ You have always paid cash for everything;
❏ You have never taken out a loan;
❏ You are divorced and have no credit history in your own name;
❏ You have never had a credit card;
❏ You have lived with your family and have no credit in your own name.

Create Your Own Credit Report

You can show a lender that you can repay a loan. You do this by establishing a *nontraditional credit history*. You will need a record that shows you have paid bills, and paid them on time, for at least two years.

To make your nontraditional credit history, assemble these documents:

❑ Keep copies of all the bills you pay: rent, telephone, utilities, car, and medical insurance;

❑ Keep copies of the cancelled checks you used to pay your bills; keep any receipts for bills you paid;

❑ Ask your landlord to write a letter to you stating how long you have rented and the amount of your monthly rent and that you pay your rent on time;

❑ Get letters from utility companies stating how long you have been a customer and that you pay your bills on time each month.

A credit-counseling service or housing-assistance agency can help you prepare a nontraditional credit history.

Should I Get a Credit Card?

When you have and use a credit card, the record of your payments becomes a chapter of your credit history. Having a credit card and using it wisely is a good way to establish a credit history. But many people have problems handling a credit card. They get themselves into debt they cannot easily repay. One way to avoid this is to understand the fees and terms. Use the card for some purchases. Make your payments each month and make them on time.

Review Your Credit History

When you apply for the loan, the bank or mortgage company will review your credit history. If you learn about your credit history now, before you apply for the loan, you will know how sound an investment you will be for the lender. Also, you can fix any errors or problems.

You can obtain a report of your credit history from three credit-reporting agencies: Equifax, Experian, and TransUnion. Simply call and ask for your credit report. You may have to pay a fee ($5 to $20). Request a report from all three agencies. Your lender will use one or all of them. It is important to make sure that the reports contain no mistakes.

Free Credit Report

Every American is entitled to a free credit report annually under the Fair and Accurate Credit Transactions Act (FACT Act). AnnualCredit-Report.com is a centralized service for consumers to request your free annual credit reports. It was created by the three nationwide consumer credit reporting companies, Equifax, Experian, and Trans-Union. Consumers can request and obtain a free credit report once every twelve months from each of the three nationwide consumer credit-reporting companies. AnnualCreditReport.com provides consumers with the secure means to do so.

AnnualCreditReport.com processes requests for free credit file disclosures, commonly called *credit reports*, at www.annualcreditreport.com/cra/index.jsp.

Experian
1-888-397-3742
www.experian.com

Equifax
1-800-997-2493
www.equifax.com

TransUnion
1-800-888-4213
www.transunion.com

You can request a *tri-merge* report. This report combines the information from the three credit-reporting agencies. Chapter 8 has a sample of a credit report that gives more information. Of course we have it on line at www.esperanza.us, where you can download it for free.

The credit report will have a number, called a *credit bureau score*. This number tells the lender how likely it is that you will repay the loan. The lender will use the score to decide whether to make the loan and the amount of the loan. Each credit-reporting agency uses a different way of figuring credit scores. Look for an explanation of the score on your report. If you cannot find an explanation or need clearer information, call the credit agency.

Review the report carefully. Is it accurate? Check each column: *high limit, total loan,* and *past due.* If you find a mistake, follow the instructions provided with the credit report. Explain the problem. You can make your claim directly to the credit bureau by the internet. If not, write a brief letter to the credit bureau and include any additional information needed to correct the error. There are sample letters included in chapter 8 and several at www.esperanza.us.

Understand and Address Common Credit Problems

The most common reasons for low credit ratings are:

- A pattern of late payments on current debts;
- Past poor credit performance;
- Bankruptcies;
- Judgments or liens;
- Past due and collection accounts;
- Charge-offs, foreclosures, or repossessions.

If your credit report shows errors that you can explain, ask the credit reporting company to add your explanation to the report.

Know How Long Information Remains on Your Credit Report

Your credit information stays with you for many years:

- Negative information: seven years;
- Bankruptcies: ten years;
- Judgments: seven years or statute of limitations;
- Student loans: seven years after guarantor action;
- Inquiries: two years.

Generally, the period runs from the date the event took place.

Solve Your Debt Problems

If you have a debt problem, seek professional help. Prepare a realistic spending plan. Consider consolidating credit card debt but keep accounts open. If you can, pay past-due accounts. If you cannot, contact your creditors and negotiate discounted payoffs, a workout plan, or a debt-management plan. If you have debt problems and need assistance in solving them, a housing counselor, a member of your home-buying team, is a person trained to help you with this problem. His or her services are free.

Seven Steps to Avoiding Credit Problems

You can avoid credit problems by taking these seven steps:

1. Apply for and open new accounts only as needed.
2. Manage your credit cards responsibly.
3. Reestablish credit if you have had problems.
4. Correct any mistakes on your credit reports.
5. Keep paying all of your bills on time.
6. Do not take on any more debt.
7. Avoid identity theft.

Reduce Your Risk of Identity Theft

Many people have had their identity stolen. Be cautious about revealing personal information. We have found that your personal information can be used by others to purchase items in your name with your credit. Many people who have been victims of identity theft do not know it until thousands of dollars' worth of merchandise has been fraudulently purchased. It sometimes takes years to rectify their financial records. Don't let this happen to you. Give your social security number to companies only as needed. Shred documents that you do not need that contain personal information. Keep your mail safe. Store your personal documents in a safe place. Do not carry extra credit cards or paperwork. Create unique passwords and PINs for accounts. Examine your bills carefully. Order a credit report once a year.

If you have been a victim of identity theft, contact the fraud department of each credit-reporting agency. Contact all affected creditors. File a police report. A sample of a letter reporting identity theft to the credit agencies is found in chapter 8 or on our website at www.esperanza.us.

Maintain Employment

The bank or mortgage company will also look at your record of employment to decide if you are a good risk for a loan. This is as important as your credit history. Your income must be stable and reliable.

Start Collecting the Financial Documents You Will Need to Apply for a Loan

- Pay stubs for the past four weeks;
- W-2 forms and tax returns for the past two years;
- Bank statements for the past two months;
- Information on long-term debts;
- Proof of other income.

4

How Do I Find the Right Loan?

Now that you have set your goals and are saving for a house, it is time to find the right loan.

To find the right loan, you will look in newspapers, check with current financial institutions, get referrals from friends and family, get information online, and work with your housing counselor.

Before you start, make sure that you know about loans and the loan process:

- Know what a mortgage is;
- Know your buying power;
- Understand interest rates;
- Learn about different kinds of loans;
- Know who the lenders are;
- Learn about special programs for home buyers;
- Know what fees you will pay;
- Know your rights and responsibilities;
- Know what documents you will be asked to provide or sign during the loan process;
- Know what financial documents you will need to apply for a loan;
- Know how to start the loan process;
- Know how to get a commitment for a loan;
- Know how to avoid predatory lending.

This section of the book explains each of these steps.

> ## Your Home-Buying Team
>
> A *loan officer* is an employee of a financial institution: a bank or a mortgage company. He or she helps you find the right kind of mortgage and works with you to understand the loan process, from your application through the loan approval.
>
> A *lender* is the financial institution that makes the loan.
>
> A *loan officer* will:
>
> - Tell you the kinds of loans (mortgages) the bank or mortgage company can offer;
> - Tell you the fees that are part of the process;
> - Determine how much money you can borrow;
> - Describe the loan process;
> - Tell you the annual percentage rate;
> - Determine how much money you need for a down payment and closing costs;
> - Tell you what your monthly mortgage payments will be;
> - Explain the terms of the loan;
> - Inform you when the loan is approved.

Know What a Mortgage Is

A mortgage is a loan. When a lender (a bank or mortgage company) gives you a mortgage, you promise that you will repay the loan and also pay the lender's fee for the loan. The money that is lent to buy the house is the *principal*. The money that pays for the loan (for the use of the money to buy the house) is *interest*. The interest is a percentage of the mortgage amount and is commonly called the *mortgage rate*.

Understand What the Monthly Mortgage Payment Includes

The lender will set an amount that you must pay by a certain date each month. This is your monthly mortgage payment. Your monthly mortgage payment includes an amount for the principal and an amount for the interest. The payment may also include:

- payment toward the local real estate taxes that you owe each year;
- payment toward your homeowner's insurance;
- monthly premium for mortgage insurance.

An easy way to remember the four parts of a monthly house payment is the term PITI. PITI stands for:

P = Principal (the amount you borrow);
I = Interest (the cost of borrowing the money);
T = Taxes (real estate taxes charged by local government);
I = Insurance (homeowner's property and mortgage insurance).

Ratios (mathematical equations) are used by banks and mortgage companies to develop guidelines for a loan. They have been developed through decades of experience with lending.

Your home-buying team will be great support in helping you understand how these ratios affect your purchasing ability. Through our interactive Internet site at www.esperanza.us, you can find out how these ratios calculate and affect you. I encourage you to experiment with different numbers at our website until you can understand the housing and the debt-to-income ratios intuitively.

Always Ask Questions

Here are two questions you might have about your monthly mortgage payment:

HOW MUCH WILL I PAY EACH MONTH? The amount of your monthly mortgage payment depends on four factors:

1. The amount of the down payment (a percentage of the purchase price);
2. The amount of your mortgage (the balance after the down payment);

Housing Ratio

The housing ratio ranges from 28 to 33 percent

The housing or front-end ratio is the *maximum* percentage of a borrower's income that can prudently be used to make the monthly mortgage payment. The maximum monthly payment, as determined by the housing ratio, includes principal, interest, taxes, and insurance.

Example: Your gross montly income is $1,500. The loan you selected has a housing ratio of 28 percent. The maximum limit you should spend each month for the mortgage payment (principal, interest, taxes, and insurance) is $420 ($1,500 x 28 percent = $420).

The debt-to-income ratio ranges from 36 to 42 percent

The debt-to-income or back-end ratio is the *maximum* percentage of a borrower's income that can prudently be used to make the monthly mortgage payment (principal, interest, taxes, and insurance) plus all other debts.

Example: Your loan has a 36 percent limit on the amount you can spend monthly for the mortgage payment plus creditor payments. Again, assume that your monthly income is $1,500. The limit for the mortgage payment plus creditor payments is $540 each month ($1,500 x 36 percent = $540).

---

3. The interest rate on the loan;
4. The amount of time you have to repay the loan.

Again, go to www.esperanza.us and you will find a *mortgage amortization calculator*. Click on it and type in different numbers. You will see how your mortgage payments are changed significantly by small changes in loan amount, down payment, length of mortgage, and interest rate. I encourage you to use the website frequently so you can better understand these ratios and calculations.

Down payments may be from 2.5 to 20 percent, depending on your lender and any special programs you might qualify for. The larger your down payment, the smaller your loan will be, and you will therefore have smaller monthly payments. However, the down payment should not be so large that you do not have enough money left for closing costs, moving expenses, repairs, and family expenses.

It is important that you do not financially *overextend* yourself. Do not take on more debt than you can afford to repay and still meet your other obligations. Do not shop for or buy a house that is more expensive than you can afford. Know what you can afford. Later in this section, you will learn how to figure out your *buying power*.

WHAT HAPPENS TO THE MONEY I GIVE THE LENDER? As you repay the loan, different amounts of your payment are applied toward the principal and the interest. For the first half of the term, most of the payment goes toward interest. By the end of the loan period, almost all of the payment goes toward the principal. This process is called *amortization*.

Each year, you can deduct from your federal income taxes the interest you paid on the loan that year.

If you sell your house before the mortgage is repaid, you will repay your lender the balance due on the principal.

The money you pay toward taxes and insurance is placed in a special account called an *escrow account*. The lender saves up the money. When the tax or insurance bill is due, it pays the local tax authority and insurance company directly.

Every month, you will receive a detailed statement showing how much you have paid, how much you owe, how much is in the escrow account, and what the lender paid to the tax authority and insurance company. Examine your statement every month and check for errors. If there is anything that looks wrong or something you do not understand, contact the lender immediately. A sample monthly mortgage statement is found in chapter 8 and on our website at www.esperanza.us.

Protect Yourself from Bad Loans and Foreclosure

When you take out a mortgage, the lender gives you the money to pay the seller for the property. The lender then holds the title to your house until you have repaid it. If you do not repay the loan, the lender has the right to take possession of your house and sell it to someone else. This is called *foreclosure*.

You can help yourself avoid even the possibility of foreclosure by taking certain steps from the very beginning of the loan process:

- Know your buying power;
- Know about the different kinds of mortgages;
- Find a reputable lender and take time to shop for a loan;
- Avoid predatory lenders;
- Avoid lenders who approach you by mail, email, phone, or in person;
- Avoid extra deals that are part of the loan;
- Do not let anyone pressure you to make a decision;
- Do not take on more debt than you can comfortably repay on a monthly schedule;
- Know the current interest rates;
- Understand all the fees you will be charged;
- Insist on a home inspection before agreeing to the purchase;
- Read all documents carefully. Do not sign any document that you do not understand;
- Never sign a blank document;
- Fill in all the blanks on all documents.

Later in this section and in other sections of this book you will learn more ways to protect yourself.

Know Your Buying Power

Your buying power is the combination of your *capital, capacity, credit history,* and *collateral*.

Capital. This is the money you have for the down payment, loan fees, closing costs, escrow, reserves, and moving expenses.

Capacity. This is your current income, income history, and future earning potential. Your capacity is affected by any amount you owe, such as for installment purchases or revolving charge accounts, which lowers your actual buying capacity.

Credit history. This is your history of paying what you owe.

Collateral. This is the value of the house. The bank will determine if it is worth what you are paying for it.

In calculating your buying power, the bank or mortgage company will determine the *maximum mortgage amount* you qualify for. The lender calculates this amount by your gross monthly income (before taxes), your debts (any debt that will take more than ten months to pay off), and other factors, such as the interest rate.

It is important to understand that this is the largest amount that the lender will possibly lend. This amount may be much more than you feel comfortable paying back. A loan of that size might require a monthly payment that leaves very little money for other important expenses, savings, and emergencies. A larger loan may be tempting, but it can lead to too heavy a debt and other financial problems later. Use your buying power responsibly.

Understand Interest Rates

The interest rates for mortgages are connected to trends in the larger financial world. In general, interest rates change over time. For years, even decades, interest rates will be high. Then, for many complicated reasons, they start to go down. They may stay down, or they may rise again.

Know how much banks or mortgage companies are charging for loans. This amount is always described as a *percentage*. You can learn about local mortgage companies' or banks' interest rates by reading the financial and real estate sections of the newspaper. Or ask the librarian at your local library to help you find information about current interest rates on mortgages.

As a home buyer, you have no control over the general trend of interest rates and mortgage interest rates. But you can learn to take advantage of a current trend toward low mortgage rates and how to deal with high mortgage rates. You should also know about the current mortgage rates so you can compare lenders and types of loans. And, of course, the better informed you are, the better you will be able to avoid predatory lenders, which we will discuss later.

Start to Learn About Mortgages

There is a lot to learn about mortgages. This is a good time to start to learn some basic information about the amount you might qualify for, the kinds of mortgages, and interest rates.

Amount. The lender determines the amount of the mortgage loan you qualify for. The size of the monthly mortgage payment depends on the amount of your down payment, the size of the mortgage loan, the length of time of the mortgage, the payment schedule, and the interest rate. When you are ready to apply for a mortgage, the lender will consider other factors to determine the amount of the mortgage. One important piece of information is the *appraised value* of the house you plan to buy. When you start to choose from the houses you might buy, you will need to understand the *loan-to-value* ratio (LTV).

LTV is the ratio of the amount of a loan to the total value of the property. The house you are buying will be collateral or security for the loan. Usually, the value of the house must be more than the amount you borrow from the lender. A lender's willingness to lend you money to buy a house is based in part on the LTV ratio. Lenders prefer a low loan-to-value ratio, though it is common to have an LTV of 95 percent to 97 percent. Don't worry about doing this calculation. Go to www.esperanza.us to the LTV calculator. Your lender or housing counselor will also provide you with assistance in calculating your LTV.

Understand the Annual Percentage Rate (APR)

The lender must tell you the *annual percentage rate* (APR). The APR is the sum of interest costs, points, and closing costs. The lender should show you how when spread over the term of your loan, these various costs result in an annual rate of interest (also called an effective rate of interest). Federal law on truth in lending requires the lender to give you this information.

Learn About Different Kinds of Loans

Before you begin to shop for a loan, learn about the different kinds of loans. You will be able to make better choices for you and your family, and you will have the knowledge to protect yourself from predatory lenders, lenders that sell illegally high-cost loans.

The two major types of mortgages products are *fixed-rate* and *adjustable-rate*. Each type has advantages.

Fixed-Rate Mortgage

With a *fixed-rate mortgage*, your mortgage payment (principal and interest) is always the same until you pay off the loan. The length of time you have to pay off the loan can be fifteen, twenty, or thirty years.

ADVANTAGE OF A FIXED-RATE MORTGAGE With a fixed-rate mortgage, the principal and interest portion of your mortgage payment will remain the same, even if market interest rates rise.

KNOW THE ADVANTAGES OF FIFTEEN-YEAR, TWENTY-YEAR, AND THIRTY-YEAR LOAN TERMS When you have a thirty-year mortgage, you pay more interest over time, but because you pay off more interest than principal in the first twenty-three years, you have a larger tax deduction.

With a twenty-year fixed-rate mortgage, you will pay less interest over time and own your house free and clear ten years sooner. The monthly payment will be slightly higher.

When you have a fifteen-year mortgage, you can usually get a lower interest rate. You will pay much less interest over time, and you will own your house free and clear in fifteen years. More of your monthly mortgage payment goes toward the principal, so you build equity in your house sooner. However, your monthly payment will be higher.

Adjustable-Rate Mortgage

With an adjustable-rate mortgage (ARM), your mortgage (principal and interest) payment changes according to a schedule. Your monthly payment will be reviewed once or twice a year.

There are limits on how much the interest rates of an ARM can change. These limits are called *caps*. For example, an ARM that changes each year might have a cap of two percentage points for the annual change and a cap of six percentage points over the life of the loan. The mortgage rates of an ARM can change in either direction, higher or lower, depending on the general interest rate. With some ARMs, you will have an opportunity to convert to a fixed-rate mortgage.

ARMs are connected to certain rates, called *indexes* and *margins:*

- ❑ Some ARMs are indexed to six-month, one-year, or three-year U.S. Treasury bills. The interest rate is refigured every six months, once a year, or once every three years.
- ❑ Some ARMs are indexed to certificate of deposit (CD) rates. The rate is adjusted every six months.
- ❑ Some ARMs are indexed to the Cost of Funds Index (COFI). This index relates to the cost that a group of lending institutions pays to borrow money. The rate on these ARMs can change every six months or once a year.
- ❑ Margins are percentages that are set and disclosed by the lender as part of the ARM. The margin percentage will remain the same for the life of the loan.
- ❑ On your loan's anniversary or contracted time the margin percentage is added to the ARM's particular index percentage increase or decrease, which results in the new mortgage interest rate.
- ❑ Both the annual and lifetime caps are always applied at these review times, and they regulate the overall rate.

You can follow these indexes by reading the financial section of the newspaper. Also, your lender is required to show you how to keep track of the index once the loan is made (so you will know what to expect at adjustment periods). The lender is also required to give you a fifteen-year history of the index so you can judge how the index may change over time.

Advantage of an ARM

The interest rate on an adjustable-rate mortgage is usually lower at the start. You may have to make a larger down payment. Your monthly payments may be lower at the start, and you may qualify for a larger loan. You should consider an adjustable-rate mortgage if you are sure that:

❑ The interest rate is too low for you to ignore;
❑ Your income will increase in time to meet the potential higher payments;
❑ You will sell the house in a few years.

Disadvantage of an ARM

Adjustable-rate mortgages are often used by predatory lenders. The initial rate seems reasonable, but then it is raised to a rate you cannot afford; sometimes the payments are doubled or tripled in a short period. When this happens, the borrower can no longer pay, the mortgage is foreclosed. Look carefully at the details of an ARM. You must understand the specific parameters of your loan, your margin, annual and lifetime caps.

Other Types of Mortgages

❑ With a *balloon mortgage* you make a lower monthly payment, but a larger amount of dollars will be due as a lump sum at the end of the mortgage.
❑ With an *interest-only mortgage* you pay interest every month for a period of time before it converts to a conventional mortgage or has to be refinanced. These mortgages are rarely used by first-time home buyers and are usually used by real estate investors or speculators.

❏ With a *two-step mortgage,* you first pay the loan at one rate of interest, then, at a scheduled time, the rate is changed for the rest of the loan period.

All of these mortgages and many more are created to be flexible for the borrower's need. The more experienced you are in finance, the easier it is to purchase these products. First-time home buyers should choose the more traditional fixed-rate and adjustable-rate products on the market.

Predatory Lending

Predatory lending is an illegal activity that can lead to people losing their homes. It is characterized by a wide array of abusive practices in mortgage and home-repair lending. Here are brief descriptions of some of the most common.

EXCESSIVE FEES Points and fees are costs not directly reflected in interest rates. Because these costs can be financed, they are easy to disguise or downplay. On competitive loans, fees below 1 percent of the loan amount are typical. On predatory loans, fees totaling more than 5 percent of the loan amount are common.

ABUSIVE PREPAYMENT PENALTIES Borrowers with higher-interest subprime loans have a strong incentive to refinance as soon as their credit improves. However, up to 80 percent of all subprime mortgages carry a *prepayment penalty*—a fee for paying off a loan early. An abusive prepayment penalty typically is effective for more than three years and/or costs more than six months' interest. In the prime market, only about 2 percent of home loans carry prepayment penalties of any length.

KICKBACKS TO BROKERS (YIELD SPREAD PREMIUMS) When brokers deliver a loan with an inflated interest rate (i.e., higher than the rate acceptable to the lender), the lender often pays a *yield* *spread premium,* a kickback for making the loan more costly to the borrower.

LOAN FLIPPING A lender "flips" a borrower by refinancing a loan to generate fee income without providing any net tangible benefit to the borrower. Flipping can quickly drain borrower equity and increase monthly payments—even on homes that had previously been owned free of debt.

UNNECESSARY PRODUCTS Sometimes borrowers may pay more than necessary because lenders sell and finance unnecessary insurance or other products along with the loan.

MANDATORY ARBITRATION Some loan contracts require *mandatory arbitration,* meaning that the borrowers are not allowed to seek legal remedies in a court if they find that their home is threatened by loans with illegal or abusive terms. Mandatory arbitration makes it much less likely that borrowers will receive fair and appropriate remedies in cases of wrongdoing.

STEERING AND TARGETING Predatory lenders may steer borrowers into subprime mortgages, even when the borrowers could quality for a mainstream loan. Vulnerable borrowers may be subjected to aggressive sales tactics and sometimes outright fraud. Fannie Mae has estimaged that up to half of borrowers with subprime mortgages could have qualified for loans with better terms.

According to a government study, over half (51 percent) of refinance mortgages in predominantly African-American neighborhoods are subprime loans, compared to only 9 percent of refinances in predominantly white neighborhoods.

Ways to Lower Your Mortgage Rate

There are ways to lower your mortgage rate or to save money once you begin to repay the loan. Here are four ways to trim the amount of money you spend on interest:

1. *Choose a shorter time period, or term, of the loan.* If you choose a mortgage with a *shorter term* (fifteen years instead of thirty, for example), you will most likely pay a lower interest rate for the loan.

2. *Pay discount points.* Another way to lower your mortgage rate is to pay *discount points.* Points are *prepaid interest.* In other words, you will pay some of the interest at the time you buy the house instead of later on.

   A point is 1 percent of the loan amount. Usually, the lender reduces the interest rate by one-eighth of one percentage point (or 0.125) for each point paid on a thirty-year mortgage.

   If you and your lender agree to discount points, you might make a payment equal to one, two, or three points. When you go to closing, you will then pay the closing costs and the down payment, as you would under any circumstance. You will also pay the points. In exchange, the lender will lower the interest rate on the loan.

   The difference in the rate may seem slight, but if you calculate the savings over the term of the loan, it can mean a significant difference in the amount of money you will spend. Discount points are a very good way to save money if you will stay in your house for a number of years.

   If you pay discount points, you will need more money at closing. Some sellers will agree to help pay the points on your loan. The money you pay in points is tax deductible.

3. *Use frequent payments to reduce the amount you pay in interest.* If interest rates are high or you need to start with the lower payments of a twenty-year or thirty-year mortgage, you can still save money. You can arrange to pay your mortgage in smaller, more frequent payments. You can arrange to pay twice a month or every other week. You will pay off the mortgage sooner and pay much less interest over time.

4. *Make additional payments on the principal.* Another way to save money on interest and shorten the loan period is to pay extra on the principal each month. You will see a line for this on your statement. Also, if you can manage to make just one extra mort-

gage payment a year, you will eventually save on interest and pay the loan off much sooner. Most lenders allow prepayment, but some charge a prepayment penalty. One extra payment annually will eliminate close to seven years of a thirty-year term and save you thousands of dollars. Ask about prepayment options when you are shopping for your loan.

Mortgage Prepayment Penalties

If the borrower repays the loan before the end of the term, the lender will collect less interest, so it sometimes puts in prepayment penalties. These penalties amount to being financially punished for paying a loan quickly or for finding a better loan (by refinancing) for your family. This is why it's important to review a copy of the truth-in-lending statement before agreeing to the loan conditions. A sample of the truth-in-lending disclosure statement can be found in chapter 8. Lenders are prohibited from charging prepayment penalties on mortgage loans insured or guaranteed by the federal government.

Keep Track of the Current Mortgage Rates

Know what the interest rates are for the two different types of mortgages (fixed-rate and adjusted-rate) and for the different time periods (fifteen, twenty, thirty years). To get this information, read the newspaper or go to your local library and ask the librarian to help you find information about current mortgage rates. Be sure to compare lenders.

Keep in mind that with the current trend, interest rates will change even while you shop for your loan. When you talk with a lender, ask if you will be able to get a *lock-in* on the rate. A lock-in guarantees an interest rate for a period of time. Lock-ins are a good idea when interest rates are rising. If interest rates are falling, you will want to wait as long as possible before getting the lock-in.

Know Who the Lenders Are

Many different types of financial organizations provide mortgages. Learn about the different kinds of lenders before you begin to shop for a loan. There are five types of primary market institutions:

1. *Commercial Banks.* Banks offer mortgages on residences and business properties. If you see or hear the words *consumer lending,* this means that the bank makes loans to home buyers.
2. *Savings Banks.* These banks provide mortgages for home buyers. They are also called savings or thrift institutions. Make sure that the bank is regulated and that all deposits are insured by the Federal Deposit Insurance Company (FDIC).
3. *Mortgage Banks.* As the name suggests, these institutions specialize in mortgages. Usually they *originate the loan.* Later, they sell the loan to another financial institution.
4. *Mortgage Brokers.* These companies do not make loans. They help home buyers with poor credit find a mortgage. Keep in mind that mortgage brokers are not regulated by any professional or government agency.
5. *Credit Unions.* These are private banking organizations that offer many different services to their members. Their mortgage rates are often very good, but you must be a member. If it is possible, join a credit union through your employer, or you may be able to join a neighborhood or regional credit union. Credit unions are regulated by state and federal agencies. Your certified housing counselor can help you find a credit union in your region.

Learn About Special Programs for Home Buyers

There are special programs for first-time home buyers with low or middle incomes. If you qualify for these programs, they can be very helpful. Each program has different requirements and features, but they all have a common goal: helping more people own the house they live in. These programs are offered by the federal government, state and local agencies, nonprofit organizations, and foundations. Some programs feature low or no down payments; others feature special mortgage rates. Some programs provide grants. Others allow the home buyer to provide *sweat equity* (work to improve the property instead of cash). Some programs allow a lower debt-to-income ratio, which makes it easier for low-income or moderate-income families to purchase a house. Special programs for first-time home buyers also include free classes on the home-buying process, information on grants, and low interest rates.

FEDERAL HOME-BUYING PROGRAMS The *U.S. Department of Housing and Urban Development* (HUD) offers a number of programs that make loans available to low-income and moderate-income families. HUD owns houses in communities across the country that it will sell at reasonable prices with economical loan terms. You can learn about HUD homes at 1-800-466-3487 or www.hud.gov. You can also find a HUD-approved housing counseling agency in your region by calling 1-800-569-4287; for TDD, call 1-800-877-8339.

The *Federal Housing Administration* (FHA) is part of HUD. This agency insures mortgages from banks and other mortgage companies. With this extra assistance, the lender can offer mortgages to home buyers who are financially capable of owning a house but do not have the savings, income, or credit histories to qualify for a mortgage. FHA must approve the lender. Contact HUD (see above).

The *Department of Veterans Affairs* (VA) has programs to assist veterans, active-duty personnel, and their spouses. The VA guarantees mortgages made by primary market lenders. Contact the VA at 1-800-827-1000 or www.va.gov.

The *United States Department of Agriculture* Rural Housing Services has programs for low- to moderate-income families who want to purchase a house. The mortgage loans can be used for building a new house, buying an existing house, or improving one in a rural area. There is no 800-number, but you can contact one of its state or local offices. For its website go to www.rurdev.usda.gov and click on *where to apply*.

STATE PROGRAMS State housing finance agencies offer programs that use tax incentives to ease costs for home buyers. You can find this information in your telephone directory or at your local public library.

In addition, state and local governments offer home ownership programs for low-income families. Your certified housing counselor can be a source of information on these programs.

NATIONAL AND REGIONAL NONPROFIT AND FOUNDATION PROGRAMS Habitat for Humanity and other national and regional organizations and local nonprofits, like community development corporations, work to make affordable housing available to first-time, low-income, and middle-income home buyers. A certified housing counselor can help you find information on these programs. You can also find information at your public library.

Know the Terms Used in Special Programs

Before you look into special programs, know the difference between a grant and a loan:

- ❑ *Grant.* A grant is a gift. It is not repaid.
- ❑ *Loan.* A loan is money borrowed and to be repaid with interest.
- ❑ *Special condition grant.* The money must be paid back within a specific time, or it may be forgiven if the recipient takes specified action, such as staying on the property for a specific amount of time.

Make sure you read and understand all the information before you sign any forms.

Know What Fees You Will Pay

When you complete an application for a loan, you will pay *a loan application fee.* This fee covers the lender's cost of analyzing the application (also called *underwriting* the loan). This process includes:

- • determining the amount of risk the lender assumes in making the loan;

- reviewing the borrower's credit history;
- calculating the value of the property.

The loan application fee covers the lender's cost for your credit report, an appraisal of the property, and any other charges. This fee is usually from $300 to $500. The loan application fee is not refundable, even if you are not approved for the loan.

Know Your Rights and Responsibilities

As a borrower, you have certain rights to information and fair treatment. Know what your rights are. Know what lenders must do for you and what they cannot or need not do.

The federal Real Estate Settlement Procedures Act (RESPA) encourages home ownership. This law aids consumers during the mortgage loan settlement process and protects them from abusive lending practices.

Lenders and mortgage brokers are required by RESPA to give you a copy of the booklet "Buying Your Home: Settlement Costs and Helpful Information" when you apply for a loan or within three business days of your application. You should go over this booklet and let your housing counselor review it with you early in the loan process.

Know What Documents and Information the Lender Must Provide

The lender is required by law to give you certain information. Within three business days of your loan application or during your loan process, the lender must give you a *good-faith estimate* of the closing costs (closing costs are the costs of the settlement, when the actual sale takes place and the property is transferred from the buyer to the seller). This document lists:

- all fees that you pay before closing;
- all closing costs;
- any *escrow* costs (funds you must place in a special account during the home-buying process, also called *prepaids*).

The lender is also required to give you a *truth-in-lending statement.* You should also receive this document within three days of making the loan application. The truth-in-lending statement is a summary of how your loan will be repaid. It includes the annual percentage rate (APR), total finance charges, the number of payments and their amounts, and the total amount you will pay in interest and principal over the life of the loan. In addition, the lender must explain the mortgage process to you and give you information during the mortgage process. Do not be afraid or timid about asking questions. The lender is in fact working for you. You are paying them to borrow their money. They are the first to want to ensure that you understand everything about your loan.

The documents and information the lender provides allow you to make certain choices, such as whether you want to:

- continue to work with this lender;
- reduce the amount of the loan;
- use a different kind of mortgage;
- take a shorter or longer payment period.

You have a right to this information, and the lender has the responsibility to give it to you under federal law (RESPA). This law protects the borrower from abuses by lenders. A lender must tell you of all closing costs, lender servicing, escrow account practices, and any business relationship between the parties involved in the closing.

You can learn more about RESPA at www.hud.gov or by calling a housing counseling agency (1-800-569-4287 for your regional agency; for TDD, 1-800-877-8339).

Know That Lenders Are Not Allowed to Discriminate

Because of the federal Fair Housing Act, lenders are *not* allowed to discriminate against potential borrowers. A lender may not refuse services to you because of your race, color, nationality, religion, sex, family status, or disability. If you think a lender is discriminating against you, contact the U.S. Department of Housing and Urban Development (HUD), Office of Fair Housing, at 1-800-669-9777; for TDD, 1-800-927-9275.

Know Your Responsibilities

Just as the lender has the responsibility to be fair and provide information, so you have a responsibility to be honest with the lender. This is also true of any special programs you apply for.

- ❑ Do not buy property for someone else;
- ❑ Do not say that you earn more than you really do;
- ❑ Do not say that you have been employed longer than you really have;
- ❑ Do not say that you have more assets than you really have;
- ❑ Be accurate when you report your debts; do not say you owe less than you really do;
- ❑ Do not change your income tax returns for any reason;
- ❑ Tell the whole truth about gifts;
- ❑ Do not list fake coborrowers on your loan application;
- ❑ Be truthful about past and present credit problems;
- ❑ Be honest about your plans to occupy the house;
- ❑ Do not submit false documents.

Act Responsibly and Protect Yourself from Fraud

Be sure to protect yourself against fraud.

- ❑ Do not follow the advice of any lender, counselor, or real estate agent who tells you to make false statements about income, employment, credit history, gifts, debts, or assets. Do not follow the advice of any lender, counselor, or real estate agent who tells you to change your income tax returns.

❑ Read everything and understand everything before you sign. Do not sign any document you do not understand.

❑ Refuse to sign any blank documents.

❑ When filing a document, fill in all blanks or empty spaces. If the question does not apply to you, fill in the blank by using N/A (not applicable).

Know What Documents You Will Be Asked to Sign and Provide During the Loan Process

Know what financial documents you will need to apply for a loan. When you apply, you will need to provide these documents:

- Pay stubs for at least four weeks;
- W-2 forms and signed copies of your federal tax returns for the past two years;
- Bank statements from the past two months that serve as proof of savings;
- Information on long-term debts;
- Proof of any other income.

During the loan process, you will be asked to sign the following documents, provided by the lender:

❑ *Uniform Residential Loan Application.* A lender's way of obtaining information that will assist in considering the buyer for a loan: employment, monthly debt, savings, and credit. It provides the lender with the basic information needed to evaluate the acceptability of the proposed loan. The application includes information about the purpose and amount of the loan.

❑ *Good-Faith Estimate.* A document that discloses *expected* settlement costs.

❑ *Truth-in-Lending Disclosure Statement.* In which credit institutions are required to inform borrowers of the true cost of obtaining credit so that they can compare the costs of various lenders and avoid the uninformed use of credit.

❑ *Authorization to Check Credit.* A waiver provided by the applicant that authorizes the pulling of his or her credit report.

❑ *Employment Verification.* A form to be completed by the applicant's employer.

A sample of each of these documents is found in chapter 8. Downloadable samples at our website, www.esperanza.us.

On the basis of these documents and other information you provide, you may receive preapproval for the loan. The application will be complete when you provide information about the property:

- The address and description of the property you want to buy;
- A copy of the real estate listing of the house or a signed sales agreement.

Once you begin the loan application process, the lender will order a *credit history report.*

After you are preapproved for a loan and have found the house you wish to buy, you will give the lender the legal address and description of the property and a sales *agreement* (also called a *real estate purchase contract* or *sales contract*).

Finally, the lender will order a professional *appraisal* of the property you plan to buy.

Shopping for a Loan

Now that you have learned the basics about the kinds of loans and lenders and some basics about the loan process, you are ready to start looking for a loan.

- Compare several lenders;
- Choose a lender;
- Begin working with a loan officer;
- Schedule an appointment and begin the process of applying for a loan;
- Obtain a preapproval letter.

Compare Several Lenders, Loans, and Programs

Make a list of at least three lenders you want to talk to first. Choose these lenders by learning about their financial stability and customer satisfaction.

Begin with recommendations from your housing counselor or real estate agent or agency. Ask friends or relatives who have recently bought houses and obtained a mortgage.

Banks in your region have materials on mortgages. Get information from several banks and compare it.

Shop by phone. Use the Yellow Pages to find the telephone numbers of lenders you are interested in.

Shop online. If you have access to a computer, you can do an Internet search for loan products being offered by local and national lenders. If you are thinking about applying for a mortgage online, make sure that the Internet site has security measures and privacy policies to protect your financial information.

Look for additional community resources. As mentioned above, many state and local government agencies and nonprofit community development and housing organizations have special programs designed to help first-time, modest-income home buyers. If they do not have any programs available directly, they should be able to refer you to other special programs in your area.

Ask your housing counselor about special programs for first-time home buyers. Most communities have loan programs for first-time buyers with below-market rates or flexible qualifying guidelines. Your housing counselor can probably tell you the specifics of each program or refer you to the lenders offering such products.

Look at other sources of information. Find out what kind of loans are offered by the bank where you have your checking or savings account, check the credit union where you work, and check the listings in the Yellow Pages and in the real estate section of your local newspaper.

The following websites are good sources for comparison:

- www.bankrate.com lists national average mortgage rates and points in the ten top markets;
- www.freddiemac.com calculates the national average mortgage rate from a weekly market survey;
- www.mbaa.org publishes national mortgage rates every week.

Keep in mind that your actual loan rate will be based on several factors, such as credit score, debt-to-income ratios, loan-to-value ratios, income history, and more.

Gather Information and Compare

Next, talk to *loan officers* at the lending institutions you have chosen. Meet with prospective loan officers in person or over the phone. Remember that interest rates change every day, so call or speak with all the lenders on your list the same day. Also, make sure that this loan officer will work with you through the entire process if you choose his or her institution.

By using the Home-Buying Checklist in chapter 8, you can organize your conversations. Ask for the same information from each prospective lender and compare their mortgages. You will find a checklist below. Make sure you write down the following information:

- company's name and contact information;
- the kind of lending institution it is;
- the type of mortgage you discuss;
- minimum down payment required;
- interest rate and points;
- closing costs;
- loan processing time;
- if prepayment is allowed.

Be sure to ask about the interest rate with no points and find out how much the rate decreases with each point. Use our mortgage amortization calculator at www.esperanza.us to assist you in your comparisons. We also have a mortgage loan comparison worksheet in chapter 8. You can also download it from our website, www.esperanza.us.

Know When to Say No

Keep in mind that you are only gathering information. Be clear about this with anyone you speak to. Do not make any decisions or agreements. Above all:

- Avoid high-pressure sales tactics;
- Do not accept high interest rates and fees;
- Do not sign any documents until you are ready to.

Choose a Lender

When you have gathered information from at least three lenders, compare the items on your checklists. Which terms and options seem right for you and your circumstances?

Also, think carefully about the quality of service you would receive with each lender. Does the loan officer take time to listen to your questions and answer them? Does the loan officer take time to explain the process and the documents? You must feel comfortable with the loan officer.

Once you have made this choice, schedule a meeting with the loan officer. At this meeting, you will begin the loan application process.

Obtain Preliminary Qualification

Once you decide on the type of loan that's best for you, you may want to work with a lender to become *prequalified* for a loan. Preliminary qualification is an informal way to determine how much you may be able to borrow. You can be prequalified over the phone with no paperwork. Tell a lender your income, your long-term debts, and how large a down payment you can afford. The lender will tell you the maximum amount you may spend on a house. At this point, the lender may also run a credit report to determine whether you have any major credit problems that would prevent you from being approved for the loan.

If you speak with a lender about prequalification, you must understand that the amount you are quoted is only an *estimate*. It does not mean that the lender has approved you for a loan. Also, make it clear to the lender that you want this information only for planning. Do not sign anything or obligate yourself in any way at this time.

Remember that the lender will tell you the maximum amount you might qualify to borrow. Earlier in the process, you may have determined a more conservative amount as the amount you can afford. Keep in mind what you can afford.

It is important to understand the difference between prequalification and preapproval.

Preliminary qualification (prequalification) is an informal process in which the lender determines the maximum amount you're eligible to borrow.

Preliminary approval (preapproval) guarantees that the lender will loan you a fixed amount if you accept the loan by a certain date and meet all loan conditions. All required documents would have been submitted and reviewed by the lender. Preapproval may also be interpreted as a commitment to give you the loan if you meet certain contingencies or loan conditions.

While not necessary, it is always a good idea to have a preliminary approval *before* you go to a real estate agent. A preliminary approval helps the agent understand what you can afford and that you are serious about the purchase of a house. A hot real estate market will have agents attending first those who are perceived as ready to buy.

Loan conditions. The loan will be provided as long as you meet or comply with certain requests or conditions made by lender. Some conditions are standard for all loans (for example, you must buy property insurance that names the lender as an insured party on the policy). Other conditions may be specific; for example, you must first pay a creditor or pay off a student loan to reduce your monthly debt. Other loan conditions may include:

- Flood insurance;
- A clear title report and a lender's policy for title insurance;
- A clean termite inspection and certification;
- A survey;
- Other inspections (radon, lead paint, or water quality).

The conditions below are common but do not apply to all loans:

- Repairs that must be completed before closing;
- Additional documents that the lender wants as proof of your income or financial condition;
- The loan may be conditioned on the sale of other property you own or your ability to pay off a debt to resolve a legal problem.

Apply for a Preapproval Letter

Once you begin the loan application process, your goal is to get *preliminary approval (preapproval) for a loan*. Preapproval is the lender's commitment to lend to you if you find a house in your price range. When you are preapproved, you know exactly how much you have to spend on a house.

It is important but not necessary to get preapproved before you start looking for a house to buy. With a preapproval you are in a better position to direct a real estate agent to help you find houses in your price range. Sellers will know you are a serious buyer.

When you meet with the loan officer, he or she will spend about an hour asking you questions about your income, expenses, credit history, and employment history. Because you planned, you will be ready for these questions.

You will also give the loan officer the documents you have collected (see page 44), including current and previous rental history.

After your meeting, the loan officer will order a report of your credit history. He or she will also send out an *employment verification* and *verification of deposit*.

Now the loan office must process and review all the information you provided. Once the loan officer reviews all the documents and verifies and confirms the information, he or she will call you to inform you of the decision.

Know How the Lender Decides to Preapprove a Borrower

The lender has to decide whether you are a good risk. Will you pay off the loan? Will you be able to handle the monthly expenses of a house?

The lender will consider your *qualifying criteria*. These are *capital, capacity, credit history,* and *collateral,* which we previously discussed.

Stable income is important. "Is it probable that this borrower will be employed and have a steady income for the term of the loan?" The lender must ask this question. As one step in answering this question, the lender sends an employment verification form (EV) to the borrower's employer. The EV asks the starting date of your job, your position title, your current salary and the salary you earned in the previous year, any bonus or overtime you are paid regularly, and the probability of your continued employment. When you met with the loan officer, you signed and dated this form to authorize your employer to release this information. A sample employment verification form is available at www.esperanza.us and in chapter 8.

If you have been with your current employer less than two years, the lender will send forms to the others who employed you during the past two years.

If you are self-employed, the lender will request federal tax returns for at least the past two years and financial statements for the business (year-to-date balance sheet and profit-and-loss statement). The lender may also ask you for a two-year to five-year projection of your business's income.

Enough stable income. The lender will determine if the borrower has *enough stable income* to cover the mortgage payment (principal and interest along with property taxes and insurance) and meet his or her other financial obligations. The lender uses *ratios.* How does the monthly housing expense compare to the borrower's gross monthly income?

Money to close. Does the borrower have enough funds to be able to close? The lender will use a verification of deposit (VOD) form to check your bank statements for the past two months. You will have signed this form, giving permission to your bank to release the information. The lender will verify the amount of money in your accounts. A sample is included in chapter 8 and at www.esperanza.us.

Credit history. Your lender will want to know how you handled debt in the past. You have already reviewed your credit history report as you planned. You should have checked for and corrected any errors. You should have prepared an explanation of any problems you had with credit in the past. If there were special circumstances, your lender will take them into consideration.

Know What the Preapproval Letter Is

The preapproval letter is a guarantee that a lender will loan a potential buyer a fixed amount as long as the borrower buys a home by a certain time and the house is appraised for the amount of money for which the borrower qualifies. This is the lender's commitment to you as a potential borrower. You must continue to meet all the qualifications at the time you make the purchase. You do not have the loan at this time. If you agree with the terms of the loan and will be able to meet all the conditions, you sign the preapproval/commitment letter and return it to the lender.

A *commitment letter* is a formal offer by a lender stating the terms under which it agrees to loan money to you, the home buyer. The lender's acceptance of the application is written in the form of a loan commitment.

Understand a lender's legal reasons for denial. A lender can legally deny you a loan for the following reasons: high debt, insufficient funds, low appraisal, poor credit rating, or financial changes during the loan processing time. If this happens to you, discuss the particulars and find out what needs to be done so that your reapplication is successful.

Once you have found a house that you want to buy, you will complete the loan application process. The amount you need for a down payment will be determined by the amount of loan and its structure.

Maintain Your Good Credit

From the time you start the loan application process through closing, you must keep all financial information available to your lender and maintain your good credit. By doing this, you will also be strengthening the good financial management habits that you have been developing since you decided to buy a house. Remember to:

- Keep pay stubs and statements;
- Pay bills on time and keep proof of payments (cancelled checks, money order stubs);
- Continue to build savings;
- Do not take on new debt;
- Meet any deadlines the lender gives you.

5

How Do I Choose a House?

When you first began to plan to buy a house, you spent time thinking about where you want or need to live. Now that you know how much you can spend on a house, you can look for houses in your price range.

When you are ready to choose a house, you will need to:

- Know what is available;
- Begin to work with a real estate agent or buyer's agent;
- Look only at what you can afford;
- Keep an open mind;
- Look, look, look, and look some more;
- Narrow your search;
- Insist on a house inspection;
- Know the property.

At this stage of the process, you must be willing to look at many houses, to look very carefully at them, and to ask important questions.

Know What Houses Are Available

Your first step in choosing a house is to learn about the available houses and housing prices in the community where you would like to live.

Before you engage a real estate agent, spend time learning about houses that are available in your price range in the community where you hope to buy. By taking the time to gather this information before you engage an agent:

- You will be more knowledgeable when you are ready to choose an agent;
- You will be better prepared to work with the agent because you will have a clear idea of what you want and what you do not want;
- Your time with the agent will be more productive.

You will make the best use of the agent's knowledge and skills if you do this basic work first.

Local newspapers will list houses for sale in the classified section of the paper. Look for two kinds of newspapers. A major paper serves a region that includes a major city and surrounding counties. Small papers published once a week serve communities or even individual neighborhoods in the community. Look for real estate listings in both kinds of papers.

Weekend editions of the major papers also have special real estate sections that list houses. They also advertise scheduled *open houses*.

Go to Open Houses

An open house is just what it sounds like: at a certain time on a certain day, anyone can walk through the property and look around. The agent selling the house arranges the open house. Prospective buyers can speak with the agent and ask questions.

The open house is held with the understanding that most people will go only to browse. There is no pressure for you to make a decision or even to make an appointment for a private tour of the house at a later date.

Usually there are printed materials about the house. You can take some and study them at your leisure. Take a little notepad with you and write down questions and ideas.

Attending open houses is very useful. You will get a good education about what kinds of houses are available. You will see what kinds of features they have and what kind of condition they are in. You can use the printed information to compare several houses.

You will also learn about the different real estate agencies in the area and the kind of houses they specialize in. You will meet at least one real estate agent; often you will meet others who are there to look or have clients with them. You will begin to get comfortable with looking at a house and knowledgeable in what to look for and how to ask questions. You will begin to see things you like or don't like in a house. The more open house visits you make, the more refined your understanding will be of what you want in a home. Remember, this is one of the most important purchases you will make in your lifetime. Take your time to learn what you really want.

Use Real Estate Agents' Websites

Real estate agents' websites are a good way to learn about what is available. Go to your local library and ask the librarian for help accessing these websites. Most agents list the available properties and their prices. They post pictures of the houses. Some even provide virtual tours of the house and property. Often, you can simply enter your price range and the site will take you to the houses in that range.

Visit the Community Regularly

Look for For Sale signs. You may find properties that are not advertised, including houses for sale by the owner. Go more than once, as houses go on the market every day. By going back to the community often, you will accomplish two things: you will learn what houses are available and you will learn about the community.

Use Your Network

Tell other family members, friends, and coworkers that you are looking for a house to buy.

Learn About Special Programs

Government housing agencies, nonprofit housing agencies, and foundations renovate or build houses and make them available for low-income and moderate-income families. Work with your certified housing counselor to get information about these programs. Check with your state or city housing agency. If you need help on how to contact these agencies, go to your local library and ask the librarian to assist you.

Consider Other Sources of Houses

Other sources of houses and property include federal agencies, banks and mortgage companies, auctions, and abandoned housing.

You can buy a house from the federal government or a lending institution. The U.S. Department of Housing and Urban Development (HUD) and the U.S. Department of Veterans Affairs (VA) have properties for sale. Keep in mind that these properties are sold as is, and they are most likely in need of repair. The buyer may need a lender who will approve a loan that includes money for extensive repairs. There are also special programs for buyers of these properties: HUD has the 203(k) program, which allows the buyer to use one loan to both purchase the house and fix it up. With a house that needs a lot of renovation, the owner has an opportunity to make important energy-saving improvements with new materials and systems.

When a buyer cannot repay his or her loan, the banks and mortgage company foreclose. The lender then sells the property to try to make up for its loss. You can find out if foreclosed houses are available by contacting the *real estate owned* (REO) office of the lender.

Property auctions are another source of houses. The owner has died and left no heir or had to file bankruptcy. The property is auctioned to the highest bidder at an *estate auction* or *sheriff's sale*. Usually the buyer must be prepared to close immediately. The buyer should be approved for a mortgage before going to the auction.

A boarded-up abandoned property might not be advertised for sale or available even through an auction, but the owner might be willing to sell it. The prospective buyer must go to the local lands record office and find out who the owner is. A written offer to the owner can result in a sale.

Consider New Construction

New construction is another option. One possibility is to buy land that has no house on it. You then find a builder to construct your house. Another possibility is to purchase a house that is part of a new construction development.

If your house is going to be built, you must choose the builder carefully. A builder should give you the names of other people he has built houses for. You should visit them to look at his work and talk to them about their houses and any problems they had. He should tell you what kind of warranty he offers. He should make all emergency repairs in the first year and make a limited number of nonemergency repairs in the first 30 to 120 days after you move in.

If you are buying a new construction in a development, investigate the builder and development company to make sure that they are reputable. Visit other new developments built by this team and talk to the owners. Ask about the warranty they offer on the construction and customer service after the sale.

You can investigate the builder and development company by asking the librarian at your local library to help you. He or she can help you search the archives of local papers and other records to see if there have been problems with the company's developments or construction works.

Always ask about the materials and energy-saving features the builder will use. Then research the materials. Ask about the timeline for the work. Have a lawyer read the warranty that the builder or company offers. Find out if the builder is a member of the National Association of Home Builders.

Work with a Real Estate Agent or Buyer's Agent

When you first started thinking about buying and owning a house, you asked yourself many questions about the kind of house you want and where you want to live. You have taken the time to learn about houses that are available and you have learned about different ways to find a house. Now you are ready to begin to work with a real estate agent or buyer's agent.

Most house buyers use a *real estate agent*. A real estate agent has the training and a license to negotiate and arrange real estate sales. The real estate agent can represent the seller, the buyer, or both.

In return for his or her services, the agent receives a commission from the seller. Generally the commission is 6 percent of the sale price of the house. If more than one agent is involved in the sale, they split the commission. It is important to understand that the real estate agent is trying to get the highest price for the house.

A real estate agent works for a *real estate broker*. If the agent or broker is a member of the National Association of Realtors, then he or she is called a *Realtor*.

A *buyer's agent* is a real estate professional that represents only the buyer.

Find a real estate agent you can trust. When you are ready, here are some ways you can find one:

❑ Get references from friends, family, and coworkers. Are there agents they would recommend? Ask what they liked about the agent and what concerns they had.

❑ Learn about agencies that serve the community where you will buy. The real estate agent from the companies that serve the area where you plan to buy will know and understand the properties and the community. You can find out which companies serve the area by touring the community and noting the names on For Sale and Sold signs. Attend open houses in the community and see the kinds of properties these companies represent. You can meet the real estate agent who is hosting the open house, and you might meet other agents who are touring the property.

❏ Call your local association of real estate agents. Get a list of agents that list properties in the area where you hope to buy. The National Association of Realtors is the professional organization for Realtors and agents. Call 1-800-874-6500 or go to www.realtor.org for information about regional listings of Realtors and regional associations of Realtors.

❏ Agents can serve as a referral source to a lending institution, a mortgage company, or a bank, but it is your responsibility to search for the best possible mortgage for your house.

SHOP FOR AN AGENT Think of the agent as someone you are hiring to work for you. Interview several agents and decide which one is right for the job. Ask each agent the same set of questions and take notes on their answers. If you do not understand something, ask for an explanation. If you have a question later, call the agent.

The agent should be someone you feel comfortable with. The agent should be willing to answer all your questions. He or she should be patient and willing to explain things. You should feel that the agent wants to help you find the right house.

You should not feel that the agent is trying to exclude you from a community because of your race, color, religion, nationality, family status, or disability. You should not feel that the agent is trying to pressure you to spend more than you have decided is right for you.

The agent should be on time for every appointment. The agent should be attentive to and accurate with details. These qualities suggest that he or she will make sure that all documents are correct and that every deadline is met.

Do not agree to have an agent work for you until you are sure that you want this person to be your agent. Do not sign any papers until you have made a firm decision. Make the decision in your own time. Do not let anyone pressure you into making a decision.

Do not feel pressured or obliged to engage an agent only because he or she is a friend, a friend of a family member or coworker, or a member of your family. This should be a professional relationship.

The National Association of Realtors publishes a code of ethics. You can find it at www.realtor.org.

Lawyer (attorney-at-law). You may live in a state that requires a lawyer to handle certain parts of the home-buying process. Other states require that a lawyer handle parts of the process only if no qualified real estate agent is involved. Regardless, you may want to hire a lawyer to help you with paperwork and contracts, as they can be complex. A lawyer can review contracts with you. He or she can also help you with the closing process. Find a lawyer who has experience working with home buyers. If you hire one, know what the hourly cost is or if they have a set fee or are willing to set a price cap for a closing. It is less costly to direct your general questions to a government-funded housing counselor than having to ask a lawyer for general advice.

Look Only at Houses You Can Afford

You know what you can afford. You know how much money you have to buy and maintain a house. Be clear and firm with your real estate agent or buyer's agent. Look only at the houses you can afford.

It may be tempting to look at something outside your price range, but keep in mind that you might be in for disappointment and problems if you try to buy something you cannot afford.

You will need a larger down payment for a more expensive house, and your monthly mortgage payment may be so large that you have trouble meeting your other obligations. Also, the taxes on the property are likely to be higher. Homeowner's insurance will be higher. And the cost of maintaining the property may be higher. If you cannot keep up the property, its value will fall.

It may be better to buy something you can afford and increase the value of your investment by improving the property.

KEEP AN OPEN MIND Learn how to look beneath the surface. A house in good structural condition may not *look* like your dream house, but it may have the potential to *become* your dream home.

If the décor of the house is not something you like or is worn or not up to your standards of cleanliness, try to imagine the house transformed by your taste. Small, inexpensive improvements can make a big difference. Walls and cabinets can be repainted. Curtains can be replaced. An ugly or stained carpet may be hiding a beautiful hardwood floor. A wall that bears no weight can easily be taken down to make a room larger and brighter. A window can be added. Ugly or worn siding can be replaced.

Learn to think the same way about the surrounding property. Trees and shrubs can be removed or added.

Remember that you are buying only the seller's *structure,* not the seller's *taste.* Don't miss the chance on a house with potential.

You may also be missing a bargain. Houses that do not show well occasionally stay on the market for a long time or are priced lower than similar houses in the area. The seller may be willing to take a price lower than the asking price.

Remember, look, look, look, and look some more!

Most first-time home buyers look at fifteen to twenty-five houses before they make a purchase. You may need to look at many more, so be willing to look at many houses. Do not be discouraged if the process takes a long time, even several months. You are not wasting time. You are becoming more knowledgeable with every house you view. Also, you are saving and managing your money during this time, so you will be better prepared to make the purchase and maintain the house you do buy.

Be Organized

Be organized for every visit to a house that is for sale. Make a checklist or use the one below and make several blank copies (available to you at no cost at www.esperanza.us). Make sure that the checklist includes any special features that you need. Then use the same one for each visit. Take extra pieces of notepaper during each visit. Compare your notes on each property.

Take a tape measure, camera, and flashlight on each visit. Use the tape measure to measure the rooms. Use the camera to take pictures inside and outside the house, around the property, and in the neighborhood. Use the flashlight to look closely at dark areas in the basement and attic.

Make sure you have notes on each property that include the address, type of house, asking price, yearly taxes, lot size, age, and the number of bedrooms and bathrooms. After you look at many houses, it is hard to remember each in detail.

Look Carefully

Look carefully at the features of the house. Ask the same general and specific questions about each house. Ask follow-up questions if you need more information.

Purchase price. Ask what is included in the purchase price. For example, the seller may include major appliances, such as the refrigerator, stove, washer, and dryer.

Condition. Look carefully at the interior and exterior. Check for signs of damage, such as water stains or buckling of the walls or floors. Ask the seller or agent about potential problems, such as the condition of the roof, electrical wiring, plumbing, and the heating and cooling systems.

Maintenance history. Ask about the maintenance history of the house. Did the owner ever replace the roof or the heating system? When?

Utility costs. Find out how much the seller spends each year on utility costs. Ask how much the seller pays in property taxes.

Special insurance and restrictions. Ask if the house requires any special insurance, such as flood insurance. If the property is on a federally designated flood plain, your lender will require you to buy flood insurance in addition to your homeowner's insurance.

Find out if there are any *zoning restrictions* that would affect your use of the property. For example, if you plan to locate a business on the property along with your house, zoning restrictions may make that impossible.

Are there any *deed restrictions?* The neighborhood may have restrictions on such things as right-of-way; the appearance of the property; the number and type of structures; the addition or removal of trees, pools, and garages; and additions to the house.

Be sure that you get answers to all your questions and that you understand the information. If you do not understand something, ask again. If the seller or agent is reluctant to answer a legitimate question, make a note of it. Ask the question again at another time. If it is never answered, you should consider dropping that house from consideration.

Examine the Entire Property Carefully

You probably know what you want in a house. It is very important to look carefully so that you don't end up with things you do not want, like rotted foundations, faulty wiring, and insect infestations. Use the checklist on the next page for each property you consider.

Learn About the Neighborhood

If you are interested in a house, find out about the location and the neighborhood. How will you get to work, day care, school, church, and other places that are important to you? Where will you buy groceries?

Go back to the list you made about what you need and want in a neighborhood. How does this community compare with your list?

Pick up or subscribe to the weekly newspaper for the community or neighborhood. It will give you an idea of the activities, concerns and issues, amenities, and businesses in the area.

Talk to people in the neighborhood. Ask them how long they have lived there, what they like and do not like about the community, and what issues or concerns are important to the neighbors at this time. Ask about any changes they have seen over the years.

Go to the grocery store, the park, the library, and other places you and your family will use. Use public transit to get from the neighborhood to a place that you like or is important to you.

Property Checklist

Signs of water damage or drainage problems:

___ Stains on basement walls

___ Moss, mildew, or stains on the sidings just above the foundation

___ Stains or mildew under the roof

___ Soggy areas in the yard

___ Eroded areas in the walkway or driveway

___ Leaky plumbing (wetness around pipes and shut-off valves; wetness around main water line)

___ Low water pressure

___ Siding that is wavy to the eye or spongy to the touch

___ Stains on ceilings or walls

___ Floors that feel spongy or uneven

___ Wet areas on the joists (main beams of the house)

___ Large damp areas in wall-to-wall carpeting

Signs of rotten wood or structures:

___ Roof sags in the middle

___ Missing shingles

___ Foundation is wooden posts or sills beams directly on the ground

___ Rotted sections of floors

Signs of a shifting or damaged structure:

___ Walls curve in and out

___ Windows or doors look crooked

___ Porch leans or sags

___ Diagonal cracks above doors and windows

___ Slipping or shifting foundation

___ Uneven floors

___ Doors and windows do not fit

(Continued on following page)

Property Checklist (continued)

Signs of problems with the heating/cooling and electrical systems:

____ Very high heating and cooling bills

____ Undersized electrical service (fuses blow or circuit breaker cuts off when several lights and appliances are on)

____ Lots of extension cords and auxiliary outlets

____ Smell of gas

Signs of other problems:

____ Smell of sewer or septic tank

____ Several layers of roofing

____ Cracked or blistered roofing

____ Old, flaking paint on sills and trim in the house

____ Flaking paint on the exterior

____ Signs of termites, ants, or other insects

____ Rotted or unhealthy trees and shrubs

A downloadable copy is available on our website at www.esperanza.us.

Try to see what it feels like to live in the neighborhood. Take notes about what you liked and did not like and any concerns that you have.

Think about Basic Needs: Safety and Schools

Safety. Does the neighborhood have adequate police, fire, and medical service? How close is the nearest fire hydrant or source of water for a fire truck? Is the neighborhood safe? Are the houses and businesses well kept? Do you see bars on windows and doors and security alarm signs?

Visit the area at night. Are there signs of illegal activity?

Visit or contact the local police station and ask for crime statistics. Also, the newspaper for the neighborhood or community may publish a list of the police activity for the previous week. Read the reports over several weeks.

Schools. If children live in your household, the quality of the schools will be important to you. You might also need after-school programs for the children in your household. Arrange to visit the neighborhood school. Talk to the people you meet in the neighborhood and ask them about schools.

The school district should give you information about test scores, pass rates, graduation rates, and the percentage of graduates who go on to college.

Even if children do not live in your household, the quality of schools is important because it affects property values in the area. Families and business want to be near good schools.

Consider Taxes and Insurance

These costs can affect your monthly mortgage payment.

Taxes. Are the property taxes reasonable? What services do you get for your taxes? For example, will you have to pay for a private service to remove trash?

You can get this information from a real estate agent or the local tax assessor's office.

Insurance. Contact an insurance agent. Ask about the average cost of homeowner's insurance in the community. Ask about the average cost of car insurance.

Selecting a House

By now you have looked at many properties. As you narrow your search, use your notes and checklists. Compare the good and bad points of the properties and neighborhoods. Choose the house you want to buy.

KNOW THE FAIR MARKET VALUE OF THE HOUSE Make sure the property is not overpriced. Get a list of comparable properties in the neighborhood that have sold in the last twelve months. Review the list with your agent to see if the house is appropriately priced.

Seller's Disclosure

Ask for a seller's disclosure. The seller must complete a disclosure sheet listing every problem he or she ever had on the property and what was done to fix it. You have a right to know this information. Also, you can compare this disclosure to your checklist and the inspection report you receive from a licensed home inspector. A sample disclosure is found in chapter 8 or at www.esperanza.us.

INSIST ON A HOUSE INSPECTION Once you have selected a property to bid on, you should shop for a home inspector to be part of your home-buyer's team. You do not need to contract the home inspector till you have an agreement of sale with the seller of the property.

The cost of a house inspection is your responsibility. It may be $300 or more. But consider the amount of money you might spend on the house. An inspection will protect you from buying a house that is unsafe or that will need unexpected and serious repairs. The house inspector works for you and helps you to be as informed as possible about the property. Make this important investment.

Also, have the house inspected after you make a written offer. Make sure that the agreement of sale allows for the inspection and renegotiation if there are major problems with the house. In certain cases you might want to walk away because of health issues or the cost of health-related repairs, such as asbestos, faulty electrical wiring, or the need for a new roof. Either the seller makes cost or repair concessions, or you should be allowed to walk away from the house and have your down payment returned.

A house inspection should be done by a licensed inspector. You must look for someone who is experienced and has high standards and ethics and a deep knowledge of houses and structures. The inspector should be independent of any construction or contracting business.

Your Home-Buying Team

You will need a *licensed home inspector* to examine any property you are serious about buying. The home inspector:

- Provides an impartial, in-depth evaluation of the physical condition of the property;
- Identifies items that need replacement or repair;
- Provides estimates of the cost of repairs and of the life expectancy of the systems in the home;
- Provides a professional opinion on the structural soundness of the buildings and other features of the property;
- Gives you information that you need to decide if you are making a wise investment.

When and how to find a home inspector

You should find a home inspector when you begin to narrow your search. This way you will be ready when you decide on the property you most want.

Your state may require home inspectors to pass a test and meet certain qualifications before joining a state professional organization.

Check listings in the phone book or on the internet. Look for "Building Inspection Service" or "Home Inspectors Service."

Understand that an FHA inspection is not an inspection for the homeowner. An FHA mortgage includes an inspection. However, this inspection is for the bank and the FHA. You will need a separate house inspection.

Before you engage a home inspector, ask these questions:

❑ Are you certified by an industry or professional association? Are your qualifications current?

❑ How long have you been a professional home inspector? (The answer should be at least two years' experience and dozens of homes.)

❑ Are residential properties your specialty?

- ❑ Do you or your company make repairs? Do they make referrals? (If the answer is yes, this is someone to avoid, as he or she has a conflict of interest.)
- ❑ How long will the inspection take? (It should take two to two and one-half hours.)
- ❑ What will it cost? (The national average is $250. Prices may be higher in certain locations or for a very experienced inspector.)
- ❑ Will you give me a written or videotape report? (The answer should be yes.)
- ❑ May I attend the inspection? (The answer should be yes.)
- ❑ How do you keep learning professionally? (The answer should be through courses and study.)

What Will the Inspector Do?

The house inspector examines the property for *structural problems*. He or she will look at the interior, the exterior, and the systems. The inspector will examine the plumbing, electrical systems, gutter, roof, attic, basement, waste and drainage systems, floors, walls, ceilings, windows, doors, foundation, and any other buildings on the property. The inspector will tell you if any materials in the house are unsafe and if there is any sign of insect infestation. He or she will alert you to any potential problems with the property.

If the inspector finds any defects, he or she will suggest repair methods.

After the inspection, you will receive a formal report that presents the information in detail. This report will be written, in a video, or both. In the report, the inspector will give a professional opinion of the condition of the property.

The home inspector does *not* give you an opinion of the value of the property. However, the inspector's findings will help you decide on your offer and negotiate a purchase price.

Go On the Inspection

Meet the inspector at the property (be there early) and follow him or her through the entire property. Ask questions. If you do not understand the answer, ask the question again.

Use Your Inspection Report

When you receive the inspection report, make sure that you understand it. If you do not, call the inspector. It is the responsibility of the inspector to ensure that you understand it. As with all the members of your home-buying team, insist that he or she explain everything to you. The inspector works for you. Your housing counselor can also help you review and interpret how the report may affect your purchase.

Use the house inspector's report to make decisions. The most basic decision you will make is whether you want to try to buy the property. What did you learn on the inspection and from the report? Do you still want this property? Or maybe it looks even more promising than it did.

You can also use the inspection report to determine what amount of repair and maintenance is ahead of you if you buy this property. Knowing this will help you decide how much to offer. You will use the information on necessary repairs when, as part of your offer, you present *contingencies*. For example, you might offer a price on the condition that the seller makes specified repairs before the sale.

6

How Do I Make the Purchase?

You have found the house you want to buy. Now you are ready to make the purchase. At this point in the process of buying a house you need to:

- Know how to make an offer;
- Know what to do once your offer is accepted;
- Purchase homeowner's insurance;
- Do a final walk-through of the property;
- Prepare for closing.

Know How to Make an Offer

The amount that you offer for the house depends on many factors:

❑ Consider similar houses in the area. What have they sold for recently? They should be similar in structure, size, features, and surrounding property. Your real estate agent can provide you with information about recent sales in the area. The information is also available at the local courthouse.

❑ Consider the condition of the house. What repairs or improvements does it need? (These were revealed during the house inspection.) Your offer can reflect an expectation that the seller will fix these problems or it can reflect that you will make the repairs.

❑ Consider the size of the mortgage loan you have qualified for.

❑ Consider how long the house has been for sale (on the market). If the seller has been waiting three to six months or more, he or she might be willing to accept an offer below the asking price. If the seller has already reduced the price once or more, he or she might accept a lower offer.

❑ Consider the competition. Has the seller received other offers? If the seller has other offers on the house and you really want it as your home, you should probably make an offer that is close to or above the asking price.

If you have a buyer's agent, he or she will help you decide what to offer. A seller's agent will try to get the best possible price for the seller.

Sellers behave in many different ways, depending on their personality and their circumstances. Some sellers will not lower their asking price. A seller who will not accept an offer below the asking price may consider making improvements and repairs that the buyer would have to pay for later anyway.

When you make your offer, the seller can take one of three actions:

❑ Accept the offer. The seller agrees to the offer with no changes.

❑ Reject the offer. The seller can simply refuse the offer. Your real estate or buyer's agent should learn why the offer was rejected. If the reason is something you can address, you can make a new offer.

❑ Make a counteroffer. This is a very common response. The seller chooses to negotiate some part of it. The seller will make a counteroffer with the changes he or she proposes to make to your offer. Now it is your turn to accept or reject the counteroffer or make your own counteroffer.

It is possible that you and the seller will make several counteroffers. You have different goals. You want to get the house for the lowest possible price, and the seller wants a good return on his or her investment.

The seller's agent should know the range of prices the seller is willing to accept and the repairs he or she is willing to make to sell the house. The agent may tell you or your agent that the seller is not likely to accept your offer. But keep in mind that the seller's agent has a legal obligation to tell the seller about every offer.

Making the Offer

In all your dealings, be fair, reasonable, and honest. Treat the seller and agents the way you yourself want to be treated. To make an offer the agent should prepare a *Standard Agreement for the Sale of Real Estate*. A sample agreement of sale is found in chapter 8 and at www.esperanza.us. It is important to note that the agreement of sale (sales contract) sets forth all details of the agreement between a buyer and a seller for the purchase and sale of a property. When it has been prepared and signed by the purchaser, it is an offer to purchase the subject property. If the document is accepted and signed by the seller, it becomes an agreement of sale.

Your agent will help you prepare the offer. The written offer will include the following information:

- The complete legal description of the property;
- The amount of earnest money (deposit);
- The proposed move-in date;
- The price offered;
- The proposed closing date.

Contingencies on the Settlement Statement are also important as they set conditions that must meet your approval or else you are allowed to walk away and not purchase the house. They include:

- The length of time the offer is valid;
- The repairs or improvements to be done;
- The amount and type of mortgage;
- The home inspection options;
- The sale of your current house.

Review the contract. Make sure that the purchase contract includes these items:

❏ The legal description of the property and the complete address. This information is provided by the seller. It is also available from title policies, surveys, and public records in the county where the house is located.

❏ The amount of earnest money or down payment. You will make a deposit to assure the seller that you are serious about the purchase. Once the contract is signed, the seller will take the house off the market. If you back out of the deal, the seller keeps the down payment. If the seller backs out of the deal, your money is refunded. The contract should spell out under what circumstances the money will be refunded. You decide the amount of earnest money offered (the down payment). Your agent can guide you on this decision. The seller does not get the money directly; it is given to a real estate broker or placed in an escrow account. When you go to the closing, the full amount of the earnest money is counted toward your purchase. This transaction should be by check. No cash transactions should take place.

❏ A time period for the contract. The contract has a clearly stated time period, starting from the date of the offer. If for some reason the seller is in another town, out of state, or not available, you should ask to extend the time period to allow for delays in communication. The response to your request should be in writing.

❏ A time period for home inspection. You are usually given up to two weeks to have a home inspection. Try to have the home inspection option that allows you to walk away from the purchase of the house even if the seller promises to make the repairs. You do not want to be obligated to buy if an inspection report finds something you don't like about the house. After the inspection you can either accept the property as is, ask for a reduction in price if there are repairs that were not known at the time of your bid, or walk away from the property with a return of your deposit.

❏ Ask the seller to provide a list of reputable contractors who have worked on the house. This list can prove helpful for information on the home prior to purchase and once you have purchased the house.

❏ The bank will order an appraisal to assure that the sale price is in line with the property's value.

Appraisal

At this time, your lender will want to make sure that the value of the house is enough to secure the loan. The lender wants to know:

❏ What is the value of the house?
❏ Is the house marketable?

The lender will hire a professional *appraiser*. He or she will give a professional opinion of the house's value. Your lender must allow you to see the *appraisal report*.

Once the bank is satisfied that the property is worth the price, it will issue you a commitment letter. A commitment letter is a formal offer by a lender stating the terms under which it agrees to loan money to a home buyer.

Purchase Homeowner's Insurance

Your next step is to purchase *homeowner's insurance*. This is also called *hazard insurance*. This insurance protects your house against loss. The amount of your policy must be equal to or greater than the amount of the mortgage.

You will need a copy of the policy and show that you have paid for

Your Home-Buying Team

Your lender will arrange for the property to be appraised. A professional *appraiser:*

- Provides a professional opinion on the value of the property;
- Determines that the mortgage amount is not larger than the value of the property.

the first year of insurance. Your insurance payments are called *premiums*. Your coverage must begin on the date of closing.

Know What Your Homeowner's Insurance Covers

Your homeowner's insurance will cover your house and other buildings on the property and your family's possessions in the house. This is called *property insurance.*

Your Home-Buying Team

You will need to find an *insurance agent* who can help you choose the right *homeowner's insurance* for the property. An insurance agent works for an insurance company. He or she:

- Helps you find the right protection against loss;
- Tells you what the premium (cost) of the insurance will be;
- Explains what kind of insurance are required by your lender;
- Provides documents to prove to the lender that you have insurance on the property, scheduled to start when the purchase is final.

Here are some ways you can find an insurance agent:

- Get references from friends, family, and coworkers. Do they know the agents that they recommend? Ask what they liked about the agent and what concerns they had.
- Learn about agencies that serve the community where you will buy. An insurance agent with an agency that serves the area where you plan to buy will know and understand the properties and the community.
- Call your local association of insurance agents. Get a list of insurance agents in the area where you hope to buy. The librarian at your local public library can help you find this information.

In addition, your insurance will have *liability coverage*. You have protection if through your negligence or that of members of your household someone (*a third party*) is injured or that person's property is damaged, whether on your property or elsewhere.

Understand the Basic Types of Insurance

Before you find an agent, you should know about the different types of protection and decide what is right for your house. Your decision may be based on the climate and other features of your region. Each of these three homeowner policies will differ a bit from provider to provider. That is why it is good to shop and compare.

HO-1 Basic form. This is the kind of protection that your lender will most likely require. It will cover loss from fire, lightning, windstorm, and hail. It covers loss from explosion, riot, aircraft, and vehicles. It usually covers against loss from smoke, vandalism, theft, glass breakage, and volcanic eruption.

HO-2 Broad form. This coverage provides all the protection of HO-1, Basic form. In addition, it covers loss or damage from the weight of snow and ice; electrical surges; malfunctions, freezing, and leakage in mechanical systems and appliances; collapse of the building; and falling objects.

HO-3 Special form (also called *All Risk*). This covers every cause or source of loss and damage that HO-1 and HO-2 cover. It also covers loss and damage from all other perils. However, losses from certain perils are excluded, such as flood, earthquake, war, and nuclear accidents.

If the property you are buying is located in an area that has been designated a *flood plain* by the *federal government,* your lender will require you to purchase *flood insurance.* (You should have known whether the house is on a flood plain before you made an offer on the house. Also, some government mortgage programs will not allow you to purchase a house in a designated flood plain.) Keep in mind that after you buy the house, if the federal government designates the area a flood plain, your lender will require you to buy flood insurance.

Keep all insurance up-to-date. Make sure that your property insurance has an *inflation rider*. With an inflation rider, the insurance company will automatically increase the coverage as the value of your house increases with inflation. Make sure that your policy provides *new replacement costs*, not the replacement value. Also, if you make important improvements and renovation to your house, increase your policy accordingly.

There are other kinds of insurance for your house and possessions. *Home warranties* protect your house's mechanical systems (heating, cooling, water) and the appliances that are connected to them (furnace, water heater) for a specific time period. This kind of warranty covers repairs to the system and appliances that are not covered by your homeowner's insurance.

A *homeowner's warranty* covers repairs to a specific part of the house for a limited amount of time. This coverage is useful if you have a contractor make a large and expensive repair or improvement.

Prepare for Closing

DO A FINAL WALK-THROUGH OF THE PROPERTY The seller will sometimes remain in the house for a brief time, paying rent to the buyer (who, after closing, is the new owner). Usually the owner moves out of the property before closing. At this time, the property should be empty of everything except what is included in the purchase.

This is your chance to look at the property without furniture or other items. Check the property completely, inside and out. Look carefully at any work the seller agreed to do before the sale.

Also, make sure that any items that were supposed to stay with the house (appliances or window treatments, for example) are there. Be sure that the seller had removed all other possessions. Check all utilities (gas, electric, water) to see that they are turned on and functioning.

If you notice that problems have not been addressed or see new problems, you will have to bring this to the seller's attention *before* closing. Remember, if your purchase contract specifies that certain repairs must be done, the seller must do them.

This is your last chance to make sure the house is in the condition that it is supposed to be in.

Be Ready for Closing

Know the *date, time,* and *location* of the closing. Make sure you have clear directions and a phone number to call if you have problems finding it or arriving on time. Know how you will get there. Plan to arrive early.

Your Home-Buying Team

A *title insurance company* makes sure that there is a clear record of ownership of the property. *Title insurance* protects the buyer and the lender against any dispute about who previously owned the property.

The title company arranges for the title to be transferred from seller to buyer at a final, formal meeting called *closing* or settlement. The *closing agent* manages the meeting. He or she:

- Arranges for title insurance to protect the buyer and lender;
- Provides a record of all past owners;
- Discloses any past or current liens against the property;
- Transfers the keys to the property from seller to buyer;
- Provides a title or deed for the new owner.

Because there are no standard fees for closings, you can save money on fees by comparing closing agents. These can act as closing agents:

- Lenders;
- Title companies;
- Escrow companies;
- Real estate brokers;
- Lawyers (for the buyer or for the seller).

You may also have assistance at closing: a *closing lawyer* can help you through the process.

If an emergency will prevent you from attending the closing, immediately contact the agent and the title company and reschedule.

Know All the Closing Costs

You must also know all closing costs, both those you are responsible for and those the seller is responsible for.

A Settlement Statement (closing statement) lists all the costs involved in the purchase. RESPA requires your lender to provide this statement. It is an itemized statement of the services and charges related to the closing or settlement of the property transfer. In chapter 8 you will find a Settlement Statement (HUD-1).

Know what documents you need to bring to the closing. You must have a certified check to cover closing costs. It is advisable to have the certified check be for more than the projected cost for closing as there may be last-minute additional costs. Any overage in your certified check will be returned to you at closing by the closing lawyer or title company. The mortgage portion of closing will be either wire-transferred to the title company prior to the closing or brought to closing in a certified check by the bank or mortgage company.

The exact costs are different in each community. These are typical:

- Lawyer's fees;
- Escrow fees;
- Property taxes (to cover the tax period; you and the seller will each pay a portion);
- Interest on your mortgage (from the date of the closing to thirty days before your first monthly mortgage payment);
- Loan-origination fee (this covers the lender's costs of processing the mortgage);
- Recording fees (for the deed or title);
- Survey fee;
- First premium for mortgage insurance;
- Title fees;
- Loan discount points;
- First payment to the escrow account for insurance;

- Document-preparation fees;
- Appraisal fee;
- Credit report fee;
- Notary fees;
- Express mail or courier fees.

Attend the Closing

The *closing* is the time when the property is formally sold. *Settlement* is another word used to mean the closing. At this time, the property is transferred from the seller to the buyer.

Every locality has different rules and processes for closing. In some regions, all parties meet together in one place and sign documents at the same time. In other regions, there is no face-to-face meeting.

What Happens at the Closing?

At the closing, the buyer and seller sign many different forms and provide a lot of important information. They also pay the fees.

The *closing agent* will list the money you owe the seller. This amount should be the remainder of the down payment, prepaid taxes, and other items. You should receive credit for your earnest money.

The closing agent will list the money that the seller owes you, such as unpaid taxes. The seller must provide proof of any inspections or warranties.

You must show proof of your homeowner's insurance.

Once you are satisfied that you understand the documentation, you will sign the mortgage. When you sign, you agree that the lender can sell the house if you do not make your payments. You also sign a *mortgage note*. This is your promise to repay the loan.

At this time, the seller will give you the title of the house. It will be a signed deed.

The deed and mortgage will then be formally recorded in the land records.

Documents You Will Receive at Closing

You will leave the closing with these documents:

- Settlement statement (a list of all services provided to you and all the fees you paid);
- Truth-in-lending statement from your lender;
- Mortgage note;
- Deed or title;
- Binding sales contract (prepared by the seller);
- Keys to your new house.

Now you are the owner of your new house.

Celebrate Your Accomplishment!

Buying and owning a house is a very big and important step in your life. To get there, you worked very hard, learned many new things, and made responsible choices about your finances and your future.

As a homeowner, you are investing in yourself and your family. You are also investing in a neighborhood and the larger community where you live.

Make time with your family and friends to celebrate your accomplishment!

Welcome to your new home!

7

How Do I Protect My Investment?

Now that you have bought your house, you must protect your investment.

Why Protect Your Investment?

When you own a house, you are making a long-term financial investment in yourself and your family. Owning a house is a kind of savings account. You increase the value of the savings account by making deposits. When you make your monthly mortgage payment, you are making a deposit in your account. As you pay off your mortgage each month, you own more and more of your house (this is called *equity*).

The first way to protect your investment is to make sure that you are paying your mortgage, having your house adequately insured, and making all property tax payments.

Your investment in your house can help you *build your assets*. Most houses increase in value over time, especially if the owners keep them in good repair and participate in the neighborhood.

Do everything you can to keep your house and maintain its value:

- Make all payments and manage your finances;
- Get involved in your community;
- Keep up your property, inside and out;
- Keep your family and your house safe;
- Save money by reducing energy costs;

- Increase the value of your house by making improvements;
- Know how to work with a contractor for repairs and improvements;
- Have adequate insurance on your house;
- Know how to avoid foreclosure;
- Keep all records.

Make All Payments and Manage Your Finances

You worked hard to save for your house and qualify for the mortgage. You built your savings, you lived on a budget, and you limited your expenses.

When you own a house, you must continue to manage your finances in the same way. You must manage your money for home ownership.

You must make sure you always have enough money to make your mortgage payments each month. This way, you will avoid *foreclosure*.

❑ Make all monthly payments on time. Pay the full amount of the mortgage (principal and interest), taxes, and insurance.
❑ Read all statements from the lender. Make sure they are correct. If you see an error or have a question, contact the lender immediately.

Make all payments for utilities (gas, electric, water). If you do not pay your utility bills, your service may be cut off. Your house is then at risk for serious and expensive damage.

You must also make sure that you have enough money to keep your house in good repair, inside and out. You should also save money for emergency repairs.

After you make the settlement, prepare a new *budget*. Make sure your family shares in the goal of protecting your investment. Stick to it.

Continue to follow the real estate and financial news. In time, you might be able to reduce your mortgage payment by *refinancing*. Refinancing, though, is something you must do with care. A rule of thumb is that refinancing makes sense only if the interest rate for mortgages has dropped by more than two percentage points *and* you will still own your house eighteen months later. You may have to pay some of the fees you paid at closing, and there may be other fees. If your mortgage has a *prepayment penalty*, refinancing may not be a good idea.

KNOW HOW TO AVOID FORECLOSURE You may do everything right, but your circumstances can change, sometimes without warning. Your may lose a source of income or have unexpected medical bills.

❑ Divorce, the death of a family member who contributes to the household finances, or job loss can cut your income.
❑ The costs of illness or injury can be so high that you cannot pay other bills.

If your family has a crisis that will affect your ability to make your mortgage payment, immediately contact a *housing counseling agency*. It will help you navigate through your financial difficulties and deal with your mortgage lender.

There are ways to keep your house or at least maintain your credit standing and get your finances in order again. But you must work with the home counseling agency and your lender.

Be aware of scams and predators. Sadly, there are people who try to make money from your misfortune and take advantage of your panic or shame about the situation.

Be cautious of anyone who calls you on the telephone or comes to your house without your invitation. Discard offers that arrive in the mail or by email and ignore all advertisements that promise easy money. If the deal sounds too good to be true, it probably is.

Be especially aware of *equity skimming*. In this scam, a buyer offers to repay the mortgage if you sign over your deed and move out of the house.

Be sure that you are speaking to a HUD-certified housing counseling agency. Be especially cautious if a counseling agency contacts you. A HUD home counseling agency should provide all services for free. If you are charged, the agency may be leading you to deeper financial problems.

Most important, never sign anything that you do not understand or that does not seem right.

Home Equity Loans

A *home equity loan* is a loan secured by the equity you have in your home. Such a loan is usually taken out to pay for needed repairs. Be extremely careful when obtaining repair financing through a construction or a finance company. Such financing is usually at a much higher rate of interest than you would pay a bank. To avoid a predatory loan, be sure you understand the terms of the loan and how you are to repay it. Remember that these home equity loans are secured by the borrower's residence.

Get Involved in Your Community

The neighborhood or community your house is in affects its value. If the community is safe and the houses are in good repair, people will want to live there. They will be willing to pay more to own or rent in the area. Businesses will want to be in the community. The value of your house will increase.

Do everything you can to help increase the value of your house. Help make the neighborhood a safe and attractive place.

❑ Get to know your neighbors. Participate in community activities.
❑ Take an interest in the neighborhood. Join the community or neighborhood association. Learn about important issues, help solve problems, and take action to help keep problems from developing.
❑ Vote on issues that affect your community.

The quality of the schools in the community affects the value of houses. The better the school, the more families want to live in the community. Businesses want to serve the families that live there. Even if you do not have children, get involved to improve your local schools.

Maintain Your Property, Inside and Out

When you chose your house, you thought hard about what work you would need to do to repair or improve it. You also learned about the regular maintenance the house would need. You made a plan for maintaining, repairing, and improving your house over time.

Try to prevent serious problems inside and outside your house by giving your property a checkup twice a year, fall and spring. Fix small problems before they become big, expensive problems. For example, if fuses blow often or the circuit breakers switch off, check for overloads to the system and have a licensed electrician upgrade the system.

What should you look for when you check your house?

INTERIOR:
- Basement. Check for dampness. Check ventilation (air flow), sump pump, and other drainage.
- Living areas. Check for water stains on the ceilings, walls, and around windows. Check for cracks on the ceilings, walls, and corners. Check the caulking around the bathtub and shower. Check the attic or the ceiling under the roof for water stains that indicate a leak in the roof.
- Heating and cooling. Check for dirt and dust around the furnace. Clean or change the air filter. Have the system checked by a service person from the company that installed the system.
- Plumbing. Check faucets for drips and leaks. Replace worn washers. Check the toilet: if water is running, check the flushing mechanism.
- Check all appliances and clean under and behind them. Drain the hot water heater.
- Electrical system. Check box, light fixtures, and outlets for short circuits.
- Check for signs of insect infestation.

EXTERIOR:
- Gutters and downspouts. Clear debris in the gutters. Replace a worn or damaged downspout or gutter.

❑ Foundation. Make sure that rainwater flows away from the house.
❑ Walls. Check for peeling paint. Check for cracks in brick, stone, or stucco. Check for damage to siding. Check the trim around doors, windows, and eaves for peeling paint and damaged or decayed wood. Replace rotted or decaying wood trim or damaged vinyl trim.
❑ Roof. Check for missing or worn shingles. Check for damaged or blistered roof material. Check nearby trees: do branches rub or scrape the roof or hang over dangerously?
❑ Surrounding area. Check the health of trees and shrubs. Remove damaged or rotting trees and shrubs. Check for insect infestation. Check the soil for contamination if your property is exposed to road salt or chemicals.

Make all repairs as soon as you spot a problem. Try to stay on or ahead of your schedule to replace, repaint, and repair. Keep up with yard work (mowing the lawn, trimming shrubs and bushes, keeping trees healthy). Make sure you have the right tools for the repairs. (You can cause more damage or hurt yourself with the wrong tools.) Know how to work with a contractor for large repairs or projects that require professional skills.

Use Your Homeowner's Insurance

Know how and when to file a homeowner's insurance claim. If your house or surrounding property is damaged, you should contact your insurance company and make a *claim*. Keep in mind that you have a deductible and that the claim may raise the cost of your insurance.

Keep Your Family and Your House Safe

Your family is your most precious possession. Your house is your most valuable asset. Know how you can help keep them safe. You can also reduce your homeowner's insurance premium by installing safety features.

❑ Change the locks on the house when you move in. Make sure all the windows have locks.

❑ Install fire extinguishers throughout the house.

❑ Make a list of emergency numbers and post them by each phone.

❑ Install smoke and carbon-monoxide detectors. Test the smoke and carbon-monoxide detectors regularly and change the batteries twice a year.

❑ Purchase an escape ladder for the upper floors (store the ladder under a bed).

❑ Have a first aid kit ready and easy to reach.

❑ Check your house for fire hazards or ask your local fire inspector to check it.

❑ Protect your property from intruders. Lock your doors and windows when you are away. Trim shrubs where an intruder could hide. Light your house and yard. Stop your mail and newspaper delivery if you are going to be away. Have a neighbor, friend, or family member check your house while you are away.

❑ Consider a house burglar alarm system.

❑ Keep your important papers in a safe place. Put them in a fire-resistant box that you keep in your house or store them in a safe-deposit box in a bank.

❑ Know your neighbors. You will need them in an emergency.

❑ Invite the community relations officer from your local police district to speak to you and your neighbors about safety issues in your community.

❑ Join or start a local neighborhood watch association or blockwatch.

❑ Support your community's volunteer fire and medical emergency company.

Save Money by Reducing Energy Costs

You will spend less on utility costs by developing energy-saving habits, doing simple maintenance, and making your house more energy-efficient.

Over time, the small actions that you and your family take to save energy every day add up and save you money:

- Turn off the lights whenever you leave a room;
- Do not let the water run unnecessarily.

Simple maintenance will also help you save energy costs:

- Fix drips and leaks in faucets and toilets;
- Have your furnace or heat pump serviced (cleaned and checked) every year.

Make your house more energy-efficient with these improvements:

- Put weather stripping around all doors and windows;
- Install a timer on your thermostat;
- Put insulation in your attic;
- Add storm windows to all windows;
- Replace old appliances with energy-efficient ones (refrigerator, washer, dryer).

You can learn more about ways to save money by saving energy. Your local utility company and your state's energy agency have information on saving energy. They also have information on grants and low-interest loans for making improvements to increase your house's energy efficiency.

Add Value to Your House by Making Improvements

Over time, you can add to the value of your house by making changes to the interior and exterior, and to the property. Updating the kitchen or bathrooms, adding closets and other storage areas, replacing old windows, and finishing the basement will add to your house's value. These improvements also make living in your house more pleasant for your family.

More extensive improvements, such as building an addition to your house, adding outbuildings, or building a garage, take money and careful planning. Your community will have rules on changes to properties. Make sure you know them and that you have the proper permits for the work.

Financing your project. Always be careful that you don't overextend your financial commitments or fall prey to predatory lenders. You should work with your mortgage company or bank to ensure affordability. You will have to make prudent decisions. You may have to set aside the cosmetic (painting the exterior) for the structural (repairing a roof leak). You can use our help tools on financing at www.esperanza.us.

KNOW HOW TO WORK WITH CONTRACTORS FOR REPAIRS OR IMPROVEMENTS Finding the right professional to repair or improve your property is very important. You will have asked the previous homeowner for a list of the contractors and professionals who have worked on the property. When you move into your house, ask neighbors what plumbers, electricians, carpenters, roofers, and other professionals they would recommend. Ask the staff at your local hardware store to recommend reputable contractors. Keep a list of contractors and professionals on hand so that you are ready in case of an emergency or when you want to start a repair or improvement project.

❑ Ask the contractor to look at the property and the work that needs to be done. Ask for a list of references and places where you can see his work. Ask to see the contractor's state or local license for doing this kind of work. Make sure that the contractor has liability insurance. The insurance should cover personal injury and property damage.

❑ Talk to more than one contractor about the job. Reputable contractors will provide free estimates. Ask for the estimate in writing. It should have a starting and ending date for the work and a firm bid on the job. Do not sign proposals or estimates. Compare prices and think about what each contractor said about the work. Have another conversation with the contractor if you have questions or need more information.

❑ Once you are sure that you want the contractor to do the work, you and the contractor sign a contract. The contract should specify the work to be done, the time period for the work, the cost of all materials and labor, and the plan for payment. Hold back at least 10 percent of the payment until the project is completed and you are satisfied with the work.

❑ Some projects should be guaranteed. The contractors should guarantee the work for a time period that is reasonable for the project. If the contractor installs a product, make sure you get the manufacturer's warranty on the product.

❑ The contractor has seen the work of many other contractors. If you like the contractor's work, ask about other different contractors and professionals he or she would recommend. For example, does the carpenter know a good electrician or plumber?

Keep All Records

It is a good idea to make copies of all important documents and keep them with other household records. Put them in a file box, file folder, or a three-ring notebook.

❑ Keep your mortgage statements in this file;
❑ Keep records of your utility bills and repairs to your systems;
❑ Keep warranties and instruction manuals for your appliances and mechanical systems;
❑ Keep records of repairs and improvements and cards from contractors;
❑ Keep the documents (or copies of them), records, and information that you will need to make an insurance or warranty claim;
❑ Keep all records of payments;
❑ Keep all the information about the house and the costs of running it.

Think about the information that you received (or would have liked to have received) from the previous owner. Keep that information.

Think about the helpful information you received from neighbors and others. Keep it so you can use it again or pass it along to another new homeowner or neighbor.

You should also keep this book and any other books and materials about buying and owning a house. Store these materials in the same place as your file or notebook.

8

What Do Home-Buying Documents Look Like?

Almost all of the documents we have discussed in this book are available for you to view in this chapter. It is important that you become accustomed to them and that you understand the role these documents play in the acquisition of your new home. Your home-buying team can and will provide explanations of any of these items. The only major document that is not available in this chapter is the Agreement of Sale, which is much too large to duplicate in this book. You should know that all of the documents in this chapter as well as the Agreement of Sale are available for free on our website at www.esperanza.us. Just fill out the form and you will be able to view and download the documents.

Household Expense Worksheet

*Instructions: Fill in your estimated monthly
expenses in the second column.*

Monthly Expenses	Monthly Payment
HOUSING	
Rent	
First mortgage	
Second mortgage	
Association dues	
Property taxes	
Lot rent	
Home maintenance	
AUTOMOBILE	
Gasoline	
Maintenance (oil / lubrication / tires)	
Auto tags / inspection	
FOOD	
Groceries	
Meals out	
School lunches	
Food / snacks at work	
UTILITIES	
Electric / gas / oil / propane	
Water / sewer / garbage	
Telephone / cell phone / beeper	
Cable TV / internet	

(Continued on following page)

Household Expense Worksheet (continued)	
Monthly Expenses	Monthly Payment
INSURANCE	
Automobile	
Medical	
Life	
Renters / homeowners	
HEALTH CARE	
Drugs / medication	
Office visits / deductible	
Dental	
Optical	
CHILD CARE	
Day care / babysitter	
Allowances / kids' stuff	
Diapers / formula / baby supplies	
Child support	
INSTALLMENTS	
Car payments	
Student loans	
Tax installments (state, federal)	
Other	
CHARITABLE DONATIONS	
Church, charities	
EDUCATION	
School tuition and supplies	

(Continued on following page)

Household Expense Worksheet (continued)	
Monthly Expenses	**Monthly Payment**
LEISURE	
Books / newspapers / magazines	
Movies / sporting events / entertainment	
Gifts / parties / holidays / cards	
Vacations / travel	
Alcohol	
Cigarettes / tobacco	
Hobbies / clubs	
Lottery / casinos / bingo	
MISCELLANEOUS	
Work tools and clothes / occupational dues	
Dry cleaning / laundry	
Home cleaning supplies	
Bus fares / ride shares / parking	
Personal care (shampoo / toothpaste, etc.)	
Bank service charges / postage	
Pet care / vet / food / medications	
Lawn / pool maintenance / home security	
Savings / reserve	
SUBTOTAL	
OTHER DEBT SERVICE	
PAST DUE PAYMENTS AND CHARGES	
TOTAL EXPENSES	

Home-Buying Checklist

1. What part of the town (or country) do you want to live in?

   _____

2. What price range can you afford? _____

3. Do you need to consider schools?   Yes _____   No _____
   Specific needs: _____

4. Do you want a new home (less than five years old) or an older
   home? _____

5. What kind of houses are you willing to consider?
   Single____ Twin____ Duplex____ Triplex____ Fourplex____
   Mobile____ One floor____ Two or more floors____

6. What kind of buying arrangement are you willing to consider?
   Condo____ Co-op____ Lease-purchase____

7. How much renovation are you willing and able to do?
   A little____ A lot____ None____

8. Do you need to be close to public transportation?_____

9. Do you have any special access needs?_____

10. What do you need or want in a property?

	NEED	WOULD LIKE
Large lot (one-half acre or more)	____	____
Small lot (less than one-half acre)	____	____
Fenced yard	____	____
Garage	____	____
Carport	____	____
Patio/deck	____	____
Other buildings	____	____

11. How many bedrooms must you have?_____

12. How many bathrooms do you want?_____

13. How big a house do you need (square feet)?_____

14. What special features do you need (for example, an in-law apart-
    ment, storage, or facilities for animals)?_____

    _____

Credit Report

Sample Credit Report   Page 1 of 4

experian®

Online Personal Credit Report from Experian for

Experian credit report prepared for
JOHN Q. CONSUMER
Your report number is
1562064065
Report date:
01/24/2005

1

Index:
- Potentially negative items
- Accounts in good standing
- Requests for your credit history
- Personal information
- Important message from Experian

2

Experian collects and organizes information about you and your credit history from public records, your creditors and other reliable sources. Experian makes your credit history available to your current and prospective creditors, employers and others as allowed by law, which can expedite your ability to obtain credit and can make offers of credit available to you. We do not grant or deny credit; each credit grantor makes that decision based on its own guidelines.

Potentially Negative Items   **3**   *back to top*

Public Records

Credit grantors may carefully review the items listed below when they check your credit history. Please note that the account information connected with some public records, such as bankruptcy, also may appear with your credit items listed later in this report.

MAIN COUNTY CLERK

Address:	Identification Number:	Plaintiff:
123 MAINTOWN S	1	ANY COMMISSIONER O.
BUFFALO , NY 10000		

Status:	Status Details:
Civil claim paid.	This item was verified and updated on 06-2001.

Date Filed:	Claim Amount:
10/15/2000	$200
Date Resolved:	Liability
01/04/2001	Amount:
	NA
Responsibility:	
INDIVIDUAL	

Credit Items

For your protection, the last few digits of your account numbers do not display.

ABCD BANKS

Address:	Account Number:
100 CENTER RD	1000000...
BUFFALO, NY 10000	
(555) 555-5555	
Status: Paid/Past due 60 days.	**4**

Date Opened:	Type:	Credit Limit/Original Amount:
10/1997	Installment	$523
Reported Since:	Terms:	High Balance:
11/1997	12 Months	NA
Date of Status:	Monthly	Recent Balance:
01/1999	Payment:	$0 as of 01/1999
	$0	Recent Payment:
Last Reported:	Responsibility:	$0
01/1999	Individual	

Account History:
60 days as of 12-1998
30 days as of 11-1998

Report number:
You will need your report number to contact Experian online, by phone or by mail.

Index:
Navigate through the sections of your credit report using these links.

Potentially negative items:
Items that creditors may view less favorably. It includes the creditor's name and address, your account number (shortened for security), account status, type and terms of the account and any other information reported to Experian by the creditor. Also includes any bankruptcy, lien and judgment information obtained directly from the courts.

Status:
Indicates the current status of the account.

If you believe information in your report is inaccurate, you can dispute that item quickly, effectively and cost free by using Experian's online dispute service located at:

www.experian.com/disputes

Disputing online is the fastest way to address any concern you may have about the information in your credit report.

Sample Credit Report   Page 2 of 4

MAIN COLL AGENCIES

Address:	Account Number:	Original Creditor:
PO BOX 123	0123456789	TELEVISE CABLE COMM.
ANYTOWN, PA 10000		
(555) 555-5555		

Status: Collection account. $95 past due as of 4-2000.

Date Opened:	Type:	Credit Limit/Original Amount:
01/2000	Installment	$95
Reported Since:	Terms:	High Balance:
04/2000	NA	NA
Date of Status:	Monthly	Recent Balance:
04/2000	Payment:	$95 as of 04/2000
	$0	Recent Payment:
Last Reported:	Responsibility:	$0
04/2000	Individual	

Your statement: ITEM DISPUTED BY CONSUMER

Account History:
Collection as of 4-2000

Accounts in Good Standing   **5**   back to top

AUTOMOBILE AUTO FINANCE

Address:	Account Number:
100 MAIN ST E	12345678098....
SMALLTOWN, MD 90001	
(555) 555-5555	

Status: Open/Never late.

Date Opened:	Type:	**6**	Credit Limit/Original Amount:
01/2000	Installment		$10,355
Reported Since:	Terms:		High Balance:
01/2000	65 Months		NA
Date of Status:	Monthly		Recent Balance:
08/2001	Payment:		$7,984 as of 08/2001
	$210		Recent Payment:
Last Reported:	Responsibility:		$0
08/2001	Individual		

MAIN

Address:	Account Number:
PO BOX 1234	1234567899876
FORT LAUDERDALE, FL 10009	

Status: Closed/Never late.

Date Opened:	Type:	Credit Limit/Original Amount:
03/1991	Revolving	NA
Reported Since:	Terms:	High Balance:
03/1991	1 Months	$3,226
Date of Status:	Monthly	Recent Balance:
08/2000	Payment:	$0 /paid as of 08/2000
	$0	Recent Payment:
Last Reported:	Responsibility:	$0
08/2000	Individual	

Your statement:
Account closed at consumer's request

Accounts in good standing:

Lists accounts that have a positive status and may be viewed favorably by creditors. Some creditors do not report to us, so some of your accounts may not be listed.

Type:

Account type indicates whether your account is a revolving or an installment account.

HOW TO BUY A HOME

Credit Report (continued)

Requests for Your Credit History **7**

back to top

Requests Viewed By Others

We make your credit history available to your current and prospective creditors and employers as allowed by law. Personal data about you may be made available to companies whose products and services may interest you.

The section below lists all who have requested in the recent past to review your credit history as a result of actions involving you, such as the completion of a credit application or the transfer of an account to a collection agency, mortgage or loan application, etc. Creditors may view these requests when evaluating your creditworthiness.

HOMESALE REALTY CO

Address:	Date of Request:
2000 S MAINROAD BLVD STE	07/16/2001
ANYTOWN CA 11111	
(555) 555-5555	

Comments:
Real estate loan on behalf of 1000 COPRORATE COMPANY. This inquiry is scheduled to continue on record until 8-2003.

ABC BANK

Address:	Date of Request:
PO BOX 100	02/23/2001
BUFFALO NY 10000	
(555) 555-5555	

Comments:
Permissible purpose. This inquiry is scheduled to continue on record until 3-2003.

ANYTOWN FUNDING INC

Address:	Date of Request:
100 W MAIN AVE STE 100	07/25/2000
INTOWN CA 10000	
(555) 555-5555	

Comments:
Permissible purpose. This inquiry is scheduled to continue on record until 8-2002.

Requests Viewed Only By You

The section below lists all who have a permissible purpose by law and have requested in the recent past to review your information. You may not have initiated these requests, so you may not recognize each source. We offer information about you to those with a permissible purpose, for example, to:

- other creditors who want to offer you preapproved credit;
- an employer who wishes to extend an offer of employment;
- a potential investor in assessing the risk of a current obligation;
- Experian or other credit reporting agencies to process a report for you;
- your existing creditors to monitor your credit activity (date listed may reflect only the most recent request).

We report these requests only to you as a record of activities. We do not provide this information to other creditors who evaluate your creditworthiness.

MAIN BANK USA

Address:	Date of Request:
1 MAIN CTR AA 11	08/10/2001
BUFFALO NY 10000	

MAINTOWN BANK

Address:	Date of Request:
PO BOX 100	08/05/2001
MAINTOWNS DE 10000	
(555) 555-5555	

ANYTOWN DATA CORPS

Address:	Date of Request:
2000 S MAINTOWN BLVD STE	07/16/2001
INTOWN CO 11111	
(555) 555-5555	

Requests for your credit history:

Also called "inquiries", requests for your credit history are logged on your report whenever anyone reviews your credit information. There are two types of inquiries.

Requests viewed by others

Inquiries resulting from a transaction initiated by you. These include inquiries from your applications for credit, housing or other loans. They also include transfer of an account to a collection agency. Creditors may view these items when evaluating your creditworthiness.

Requests viewed only by you

Inquiries resulting from transactions you may not have initiated but that are allowed under the FCRA. These include preapproved offers, as well as for employment, investment review, account monitoring by existing creditors, and requests by you for your own report. These items are shown only to you and have no impact on your creditworthiness or risk scores.

Sample Credit Report   Page 4 of 4

Personal Information   [8]

The following information is reported to us by you, your creditors and other sources. Each source may report your personal information differently, which may result in variations of your name, address, Social Security number, etc. As part of our fraud-prevention program, a notice with additional information may appear. As a security precaution, the Social Security number that you used to obtain this report is not displayed. The Geographical Code shown with each address identifies the state, county, census tract, block group and Metropolitan Statistical Area associated with each address.

Names:
JOHN Q CONSUMER
JONATHON Q CONSUMER
J Q CONSUMER

Social Security number variations:
999999999

Year of birth:
1954

Employers:
ABCDE ENGINEERING CORP

Telephone numbers:
(555) 555 5555 Residential

Address: 123 MAIN STREET
ANYTOWN, MD 90001-9999
Type of Residence: Multifamily
Geographical Code: 8-156510-31-8840   [9]

Address: 555 SIMPLE PLACE
ANYTOWN, MD 90002-7777
Type of Residence: Single family
Geographical Code: 8-175810-33-8840

Address: 999 HIGH DRIVE APT 15B
ANYTOWN, MD 90003-5555
Type of Residence: Apartment complex
Geographical Code: 0-156510-31-8840

Personal Information:
Personal information associated with your history that has been reported to Experian by you, your creditors and other sources.

May include name and Social Security number variations, employers, telephone numbers, etc. Experian lists all variations so you know what is being reported to us as belonging to you.

Address Information:
Your current address and previous address(es)

Your Personal Statement   [10]

No general personal statements appear on your report.

Personal statement:
Any personal statement that you added to your report appears here.

Note - statements remain as part of the report for 2 years and display to anyone who has permission to review your report.

Important Message From Experian   back to top

By law, we cannot disclose certain medical information (relating to physical, mental, or behavioral health or condition). Although we do not generally collect such information, it could appear in the name of a data furnisher (i.e., "Cancer Center") that reports your payment history to us. If so, those names display in your report, but in reports to others they display only as MEDICAL PAYMENT DATA. Consumer statements included on your report at your request that contain medical information are disclosed to others.

Contacting Us   back to top

Contact address and phone number for your area will display here.

Sample Letters

CREDIT-REPORTING COMPANY

Date
Your name
Your address
Your city, state, zip code
Phone#: _____
SS#: _____

Experian Credit Report
National Consumer Assistance Center
P.O. Box 2002
Allen, TX 75013

Dear Credit Bureau:

This letter is a formal request to correct inaccurate information in my credit file maintained by your organization. The item listed below is completely [inaccurate, incorrect, incomplete, erroneous, misleading, outdated] and is a very serious error in reporting.

Line item(s):
1.   List item.
2.   List other items.

Under the federal Fair Credit Reporting Act, credit-reporting agencies are required to maintain and report only 100% accurate credit information and to investigate any claims for inaccuracy within thirty days of receiving such claim(s).

If after your investigation, you find my claim to be valid and accurate, I request that you immediately [delete, correct, update] the item(s) and supply me with a corrected credit profile. On the other hand, if your investigation shows the information to be accurate, I respectfully request that you provide me with proof of the accuracy of the item(s) in question. Additionally, within fifteen days of the completion of your investigation, please forward to me a description of the procedures used to determine the accuracy and completeness of the item(s) in question.

Sincerely,

IDENTITY THEFT

Date
Your name
Your address
Your city, state, zip code

Complaint Department
Name of Consumer Reporting Company
Address
City, state, zip code

Dear Sir or Madam:

I am a victim of identity theft. I am writing to request that you block the following fraudulent information in my file. This information does not relate to any transaction that I have made. The items also are circled on the attached copy of the report I received. [Identify item(s) to be blocked by name of source, such as creditors or a tax court, and identify the type of item(s), such as a credit account or judgment.]

Enclosed is a copy of the law-enforcement report regarding the theft of my identity. Please let me know if you need any other information from me to block this information on my credit report.

Sincerely,

Your name
[Phone#]
[SS#]

Enclosures: [List what you are enclosing.]

Uniform Residential Loan Application

Uniform Residential Loan Application

This application is designed to be completed by the applicant(s) with the Lender's assistance. Applicants should complete this form as "Borrower" or "Co-Borrower," as applicable. Co-Borrower information must also be provided (and the appropriate box checked) when ☐ the income or assets of a person other than the "Borrower" (including the Borrower's spouse) will be used as a basis for loan qualification or ☐ the income or assets of the Borrower's spouse will not be used as a basis for loan qualification, but his or her liabilities must be considered because the Borrower resides in a community property state, the security property is located in a community property state, or the Borrower is relying on other property located in a community property state as a basis for repayment of the loan.

I. TYPE OF MORTGAGE AND TERMS OF LOAN

Mortgage Applied for:	☐ VA ☐ FHA	☐ Conventional ☐ USDA/Rural Housing Service	☐ Other (explain):	Agency Case Number	Lender Case Number

Amount $	Interest Rate %	No. of Months	Amortization Type:	☐ Fixed Rate ☐ GPM	☐ Other (explain): ☐ ARM (type):

II. PROPERTY INFORMATION AND PURPOSE OF LOAN

Subject Property Address (street, city, state, & ZIP)	No. of Units

Legal Description of Subject Property (attach description if necessary)
Year Built

Purpose of Loan	☐ Purchase ☐ Refinance	☐ Construction ☐ Construction-Permanent	☐ Other (explain):	Property will be: ☐ Primary Residence ☐ Secondary Residence ☐ Investment

Complete this line if construction or construction-permanent loan.

Year Lot Acquired	Original Cost $	Amount Existing Liens $	(a) Present Value of Lot $	(b) Cost of Improvements $	Total (a + b) $

Complete this line if this is a refinance loan.

Year Acquired	Original Cost $	Amount Existing Liens $	Purpose of Refinance	Describe Improvements ☐ made ☐ to be made Cost: $

Title will be held in what Name(s)	Manner in which Title will be held	Estate will be held in: ☐ Free Simple ☐ Leasehold (show expiration date)

Source of Down Payment, Settlement Charges and/or Subordinate Financing (explain)

III. BORROWER INFORMATION

	Borrower	Co-Borrower
Borrower's Name (include Jr. or Sr. if applicable)		Co-Borrower's Name (include Jr. or Sr. if applicable)

Social Security Number	Home Phone (incl. area code)	DOB (MM/DD/YYYY)	Yrs. School	Social Security Number	Home Phone (incl. area code)	DOB (MM/DD/YYYY)	Yrs. School

☐ Married ☐ Separated	☐ Unmarried (include single, divorced, widowed)	Dependents (not listed by Borrower) no. ages	☐ Married ☐ Separated	☐ Unmarried (include single, divorced, widowed)	Dependents (not listed by Borrower) no. ages

Present Address (street, city, state, ZIP)   ☐ Own ☐ Rent _____ No. Yrs.   Present Address (street, city, state, ZIP)   ☐ Own ☐ Rent _____ No. Yrs.

Mailing Address, if different from Present Address   Mailing Address, if different from Present Address

If residing at present address for less than two years, complete the following:

Former Address (street, city, state, ZIP) _____ No. Yrs.   Former Address (street, city, state, ZIP) _____ No. Yrs.
☐ Own ☐ Rent   ☐ Own ☐ Rent

IV. EMPLOYMENT INFORMATION

	Borrower		Co-Borrower	
Name & Address of Employer	☐ Self Employed	Yrs. on this job	☐ Self Employed	Yrs. on this job
		Yrs. employed in this line of work/profession		Yrs. employed in this line of work/profession
Position/Title/Type of Business	Business Phone (incl. area code)		Position/Title/Type of Business	Business Phone (incl. area code)

If employed in current position for less than two years or if currently employed in more than one position, complete the following:

	Borrower		Co-Borrower	
Name & Address of Employer	☐ Self Employed	Dates (from – to)	☐ Self Employed	Dates (from – to)
		Monthly Income $		Monthly Income $
Position/Title/Type of Business	Business Phone (incl. area code)		Position/Title/Type of Business	Business Phone (incl. area code)
Name & Address of Employer	☐ Self Employed	Dates (from – to)	☐ Self Employed	Dates (from – to)
		Monthly Income $		Monthly income $
Position/Title/Type of Business	Business Phone (incl. area code)		Position/Title/Type of Business	Business Phone (incl. area code)

Freddie Mac Form 65   01/04   Page 1 of 4   Fannie Mae Form 1003   01/04

Uniform Residential Loan Application (continued)

V. MONTHLY INCOME AND COMBINED HOUSING EXPENSE INFORMATION

Gross Monthly Income	Borrower	Co-Borrower	Total	Combined Monthly Housing Expense	Present	Proposed
Base Empl. Income*	$	$	$	Rent	$	
Overtime				First Mortgage (P&I)		$
Bonuses				Other Financing (P&I)		
Commissions				Hazard Insurance		
Dividends/Interest				Real Estate Taxes		
Net Rental Income				Mortgage Insurance		
Other (before completing, see the notice in "describe other income" below)				Homeowner Assn. Dues		
				Other:		
Total	$	$	$	Total	$	$

* Self Employed Borrower(s) may be required to provide additional documentation such as tax returns and financial statements.

Describe Other Income   Notice: Alimony, child support, or separate maintenance income need not be revealed if the
Borrower (B) or Co-Borrower (C) does not choose to have it considered for repaying this loan.

B/C		Monthly Amount
		$

VI. ASSETS AND LIABILITIES

This Statement and any applicable supporting schedules may be completed jointly by both married and unmarried Co-Borrowers if their assets and liabilities are sufficiently joined so that the Statement can be meaningfully and fairly presented on a combined basis; otherwise, separate Statements and Schedules are required. If the Co-Borrower section was completed about a spouse, this Statement and supporting schedules must be completed about that spouse also.

Completed ☐ Jointly ☐ Not Jointly

ASSETS	Cash or Market Value	Liabilities and Pledged Assets. List the creditor's name, address and account number for all outstanding debts, including automobile loans, revolving charge accounts, real estate loans, alimony, child support, stock pledges, etc. Use continuation sheet, if necessary. Indicate by (*) those liabilities which will be satisfied upon sale of real estate owned or upon refinancing of the subject property.		
Description		LIABILITIES	Monthly Payment & Months Left to Pay	Unpaid Balance
Cash deposit toward purchase held by:	$	Name and address of Company	$ Payment/Months	$
List checking and savings accounts below				
Name and address of Bank, S&L, or Credit Union				
		Acct. no.		
		Name and address of Company	$ Payment/Months	$
Acct. no.				
Name and address of Bank, S&L, or Credit Union	$			

Acct. no.
Name and address of Bank, S&L, or Credit Union

Acct. no.
Name and address of Bank, S&L, or Credit Union

Acct. no.
Stocks & Bonds (Company name/number $
& description)

Life insurance net cash value $

Face amount: $

Subtotal Liquid Assets

Real estate owned (enter market value $
from schedule of real estate owned)

Vested interest in retirement fund $

Net worth of business(es) owned $
(attach financial statement)

Automobiles owned (make and year) $

Other Assets (itemize) $

Total Assets a. $

Acct. no. $ Payment/Months
Name and address of Company

Acct. no. $ Payment/Months
Name and address of Company

Acct. no. $ Payment/Months
Name and address of Company

Acct. no. $ Payment/Months
Name and address of Company

Acct. no. $ Payment/Months
Name and address of Company

Alimony/Child Support/Separate Maintenance $
Payments Owed to.

Job-Related Expense (child care, union dues, etc.) $

Total Monthly Payments

Net Worth $
(a minus b)

Total Liabilities b. $

Freddie Mac Form 65   01/04   Page 2 of 4   Fannie Mae Form 1003   01/04

Uniform Residential Loan Application (continued)

VI. ASSETS AND LIABILITIES (cont.)

Schedule of Real Estate Owned (If additional properties are owned, use continuation sheet.)

Property Address (enter S if sold, PS if pending sale or R if rental being held for income)

	Type of Property	Present Market Value	Amount of Mortgages & Liens	Gross Rental Income	Mortgage Payments	Insurance, Maintenance, Taxes & Misc.	Net Rental Income
		$	$	$	$	$	$
Totals		$	$	$	$	$	$

List any additional names under which credit has previously been received and indicate appropriate creditor name(s) and account number(s):

Alternate Name	Creditor Name	Account Number

VII. DETAILS OF TRANSACTION

a. Purchase price $

b. Alterations, improvements, repairs

c. Land (if acquired separately)

d. Refinance (incl. debts to be paid off)

e. Estimated prepaid items

f. Estimated closing costs

g. PMI, MIP, Funding Fee

h. Discount (if Borrower will pay)

i. Total costs (add items a through h)

j. Subordinate financing

k. Borrower's closing costs paid by Seller

l. Other Credits (explain)

m. Loan amount (exclude PMI, MIP, Funding Fee financed)

n. PMI, MIP, Funding Fee financed

o. Loan amount (add m & n)

VIII. DECLARATIONS

If you answer "Yes" to any questions a through i, please use continuation sheet for explanation.

	Borrower Yes	Borrower No	Co-Borrower Yes	Co-Borrower No
a. Are there any outstanding judgments against you?	☐	☐	☐	☐
b. Have you been declared bankrupt within the past 7 years?	☐	☐	☐	☐
c. Have you had property foreclosed upon or given title or deed in lieu thereof in the last 7 years?	☐	☐	☐	☐
d. Are you a party to a lawsuit?	☐	☐	☐	☐
e. Have you directly or indirectly been obligated on any loan which resulted in foreclosure, transfer of title in lieu of foreclosure, or judgment? (This would include such loans as home mortgage loans, SBA loans, home improvement loans, educational loans, manufactured (mobile) home loans, any mortgage, financial obligation, bond, or loan guarantee. If "Yes," provide details, including date, name, and address of Lender, FHA or VA case number, if any, and reasons for the action.)	☐	☐	☐	☐
f. Are you presently delinquent or in default on any Federal debt or any other loan, mortgage, financial obligation, bond, or loan guarantee? If "Yes," give details as described in the preceding question.	☐	☐	☐	☐
g. Are you obligated to pay alimony, child support, or separate maintenance?	☐	☐	☐	☐
h. Is any part of the down payment borrowed?	☐	☐	☐	☐
i. Are you a co-maker or endorser on a note?	☐	☐	☐	☐
j. Are you a U.S. citizen?	☐	☐	☐	☐
k. Are you a permanent resident alien?	☐	☐	☐	☐
l. Do you intend to occupy the property as your primary residence? If "Yes," complete question m below.	☐	☐	☐	☐
m. Have you had an ownership interest in a property in the last three years?	☐	☐	☐	☐

p. Cash from/to Borrower
(subtract j, k, l & o from i)

(1) What type of property did you own—principal residence (PR), second home (SH), or investment property (IP)?

(2) How did you hold title to the home—solely by yourself (S), jointly with your spouse (SP), or jointly with another person (O)?

IX. ACKNOWLEDGMENT AND AGREEMENT

Each of the undersigned specifically represents to Lender and to Lender's actual or potential agents, brokers, processors, attorneys, insurers, servicers, successors and assigns and agrees and acknowledges that: (1) the information provided in this application is true and correct as of the date set forth opposite my signature and that any intentional or negligent misrepresentation of this information contained in this application may result in civil liability, including monetary damages, to any person who may suffer any loss due to reliance upon any misrepresentation that I have made on this application, and/or in criminal penalties including, but not limited to, fine or imprisonment or both under the provisions of Title 18, United States Code, Sec. 1001, et seq.; (2) the loan requested pursuant to this application (the "Loan") will be secured by a mortgage or deed of trust on the property described herein; (3) the property will not be used for any illegal or prohibited purpose or use; (4) all statements made in this application are made for the purpose of obtaining a residential mortgage loan; (5) the property will be occupied as indicated herein; (6) any owner or servicer of the Loan may verify or reverify any information contained in the application from any source named in this application, and Lender, its successors or assigns may retain the original and/or an electronic record of this application, even if the Loan is not approved; (7) the Lender and its agents, brokers, insurers, servicers, successors and assigns may continuously rely on the information contained in the application, and I am obligated to amend and/or supplement the information provided in this application if any of the material facts that I have represented herein should change prior to closing of the Loan; (8) in the event that my payments on the Loan become delinquent, the owner or servicer of the Loan may, in addition to any other rights and remedies that it may have relating to such delinquency, report my name and account information to one or more consumer credit reporting agencies; (9) ownership of the Loan and/or administration of the Loan account may be transferred with such notice as may be required by law; (10) neither Lender nor its agents, brokers, insurers, servicers, successors or assigns has made any representation or warranty, express or implied, to me regarding the property or the condition or value of the property; and (11) my transmission of this application as an "electronic record" containing my "electronic signature," as those terms are defined in applicable federal and/or state laws (excluding audio and video recordings), or my facsimile transmission of this application containing a facsimile of my signature, shall be as effective, enforceable and valid as if a paper version of this application were delivered containing my original written signature.

Borrower's Signature   Date
X

Co-Borrower's Signature   Date
X

X. INFORMATION FOR GOVERNMENT MONITORING PURPOSES

The following information is requested by the Federal Government for certain types of loans related to a dwelling in order to monitor the lender's compliance with equal credit opportunity, fair housing and home mortgage disclosure laws. You are not required to furnish this information, but are encouraged to do so. The law provides that a lender may not discriminate neither on the basis of this information, nor on whether you choose to furnish it. If you furnish the information, please provide both ethnicity and race. For race, you may check more than one designation. If you do not furnish ethnicity, race, or sex, under Federal regulations, this lender is required to note the information on the basis of visual observation or surname. If you do not wish to furnish the information, please check the box below. (Lender must review the above material to assure that the disclosures satisfy all requirements to which the lender is subject under applicable state law for the particular type of loan applied for.)

BORROWER	☐ I do not wish to furnish this information.	CO-BORROWER	☐ I do not wish to furnish this information.
Ethnicity:	☐ Hispanic or Latino ☐ Not Hispanic or Latino	Ethnicity:	☐ Hispanic or Latino ☐ Not Hispanic or Latino
Race:	☐ American Indian or Alaska Native ☐ Asian ☐ Black or African American	Race:	☐ American Indian or Alaska Native ☐ Asian ☐ Black or African American
	☐ Native Hawaiian or Other Pacific Islander ☐ White		☐ Native Hawaiian or Other Pacific Islander ☐ White
Sex:	☐ Female ☐ Male	Sex:	☐ Female ☐ Male

To be Completed by Interviewer   Interviewer's Name (print or type)
This application was taken by:
☐ Face-to-face interview
☐ Mail   Interviewer's Signature   Date
☐ Telephone
☐ Internet   Interviewer's Phone Number (incl. area code)

Name and Address of Interviewer's Employer

Freddie Mac Form 65   01/04   Page 3 of 4   Fannie Mae Form 1003   01/04

Uniform Residential Loan Application (continued)

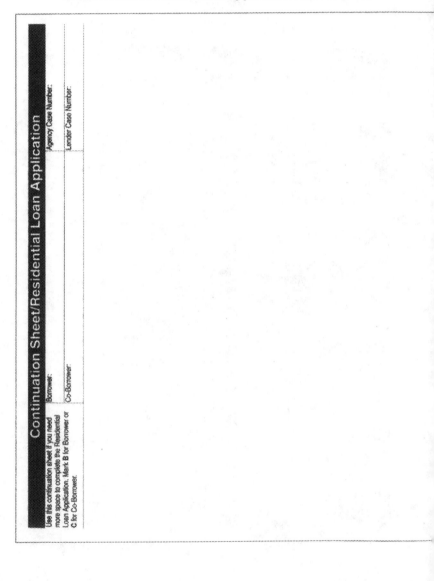

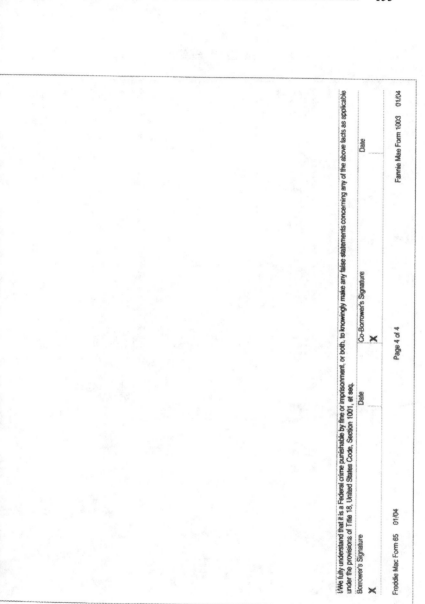

I/We fully understand that it is a Federal crime punishable by fine or imprisonment, or both, to knowingly make any false statements concerning any of the above facts as applicable under the provisions of Title 18, United States Code, Section 1001, et seq.

Borrower's Signature   Date   Co-Borrower's Signature   Date

X   X

Freddie Mac Form 65   01/04   Page 4 of 4   Fannie Mae Form 1003   01/04

Good-Faith Estimate

Lender:
Address:
Applicant(s):

Property Address:

Sales Price:
Base Loan Amount:
Total Loan Amount:
Interest Rate:
Type of Loan:
Preparation Date:
Loan Number:

The information provided below reflects estimates of the charges which you are likely to incur at the settlement of your loan. The fees listed are estimates - actual charges may be more or less. Your transaction may not involve a fee for every item listed. The numbers listed beside the estimates generally correspond to the numbered lines contained in the HUD-1 or HUD-1A settlement statement which you will be receiving at settlement. The HUD-1 or HUD-1A settlement statement will show you the actual cost for items paid at settlement.

800 ITEMS PAYABLE IN CONNECTION WITH LOAN:

801	Origination Fee @ % + $	$
802	Discount Fee @ % + $	$
803	Appraisal Fee	$
804	Credit Report	$
805	Lender's Inspection Fee	$
806	Mortgage Insurance Application Fee	$
807	Assumption Fee	$
808	Mortgage Broker Fee	$
810	Tax Related Service Fee	$
811	Application Fee	$
812	Commitment Fee	$
813	Lender's Rate Lock-In Fee	$
814	Processing Fee	$
815	Underwriting Fee	$
816	Wire Transfer Fee	$

900 ITEMS REQUIRED BY LENDER TO BE PAID IN ADVANCE:

901	Interest for days @ $ /day	$
902	Mortgage Insurance Premium	$
903	Hazard Insurance Premium	$
904	County Property Taxes	$
905	Flood Insurance	$

1000 RESERVES DEPOSITED WITH LENDER:

1001	Hazard Ins. Mo. @$ Per Mo.	$

1100 TITLE CHARGES:

1101	Closing or Escrow Fee	$
1102	Abstract or Title Search	$
1103	Title Examination	$
1105	Document Preparation Fee	$
1106	Notary Fee	$
1107	Attorney's Fee	$
1108	Title Insurance	$

1200 GOVERNMENT RECORDING AND TRANSFER CHARGES:

1201	Recording Fee	$
1202	City/County Tax/Stamps	$
1203	State Tax/Stamps	$
1204	Intangible Tax	$

1300 ADDITIONAL SETTLEMENT CHARGES:

1301	Survey	$
1302	Pest Inspection	$

1006 Flood Insurance $ _____

"S"/"B" designates those costs to be paid by Seller/Broker.

TOTAL ESTIMATED MONTHLY PAYMENT

Principal & Interest $ _____
Real Estate Taxes _____
Hazard Insurance _____
Flood Insurance _____
Mortgage Insurance _____
Other $ _____

TOTAL MONTHLY PAYMENT $ _____

TOTAL ESTIMATED SETTLEMENT CHARGES: $ _____

"A" designates those costs affecting APR.

TOTAL ESTIMATED FUNDS NEEDED TO CLOSE:

Down Payment $ _____
Estimated Closing Costs $ _____
Estimated Prepaid Items / Reserves $ _____
Total Paid Items (Subtract) $ _____
Other $ _____

CASH FROM BORROWER $ _____

THIS SECTION IS COMPLETED ONLY IF A PARTICULAR PROVIDER OF SERVICE IS REQUIRED. Listed below are providers of service which we required you to use. The charges indicated in the Good Faith Estimate above are based upon the corresponding charge of the below designated providers.

ITEM NO.	NAME & ADDRESS OF PROVIDER	TELEPHONE NO.	NATURE OF RELATIONSHIP

These estimates are provided pursuant to the Real Estate Settlement Procedures Act of 1974, as amended (RESPA). Additional information can be found in the HUD Special Information Booklet, which is to be provided to you by your mortgage broker or lender, if your application is to purchase residential property and the Lender will take a first lien on the property.

_____ Applicant _____ Date

_____ Applicant _____ Date

☐ This Good Faith Estimate is being provided by a mortgage broker, and no lender has yet been obtained.

GENESIS 2000, INC. * V9.3/W11.0 * (818) 223-3260   Page 1 of 1   Form GFE2 (03/95)

Truth-in-Lending Disclosure Statement

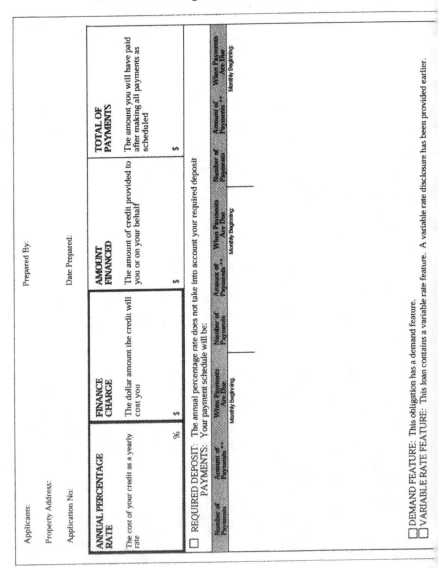

Applicants:

Property Address:

Application No:

Prepared By:

Date Prepared:

ANNUAL PERCENTAGE RATE	FINANCE CHARGE	AMOUNT FINANCED	TOTAL OF PAYMENTS
The cost of your credit as a yearly rate	The dollar amount the credit will cost you	The amount of credit provided to you or on your behalf	The amount you will have paid after making all payments as scheduled
%	$	$	$

☐ REQUIRED DEPOSIT: The annual percentage rate does not take into account your required deposit

PAYMENTS: Your payment schedule will be:

Number of Payments	Amount of Payments +	When Payments Are Due	Number of Payments	Amount of Payments +	When Payments Are Due	Number of Payments	Amount of Payments +	When Payments Are Due
		Monthly Beginning			Monthly Beginning			Monthly Beginning

☐ DEMAND FEATURE: This obligation has a demand feature.
☐ VARIABLE RATE FEATURE: This loan contains a variable rate feature. A variable rate disclosure has been provided earlier.

CREDIT LIFE/CREDIT DISABILITY: Credit life insurance and credit disability insurance are not required to obtain credit, and will not be provided unless you sign and agree to pay the additional cost.

Type	Premium	Signature
Credit Life		I want credit life insurance. Signature:
Credit Disability		I want credit disability insurance. Signature:
Credit Life and Disability		I want credit life and disability insurance. Signature:

INSURANCE: The following insurance is required to obtain credit:
☐ Credit life insurance ☐ Credit disability ☐ Property insurance ☐ Flood insurance
You may obtain the insurance from anyone you want that is acceptable to creditor
☐ If you purchase ☐ property ☐ flood insurance from creditor you will pay $_____ for a one year term.

SECURITY: You are giving a security interest in:
☐ The goods or property being purchased ☐ Real property you already own.

FILING FEES: $_____

LATE CHARGE: if a payment is more than _____ days late, you will be charged _____ % of the payment

PREPAYMENT: If you pay off early, you
☐ may ☐ will not have to pay a penalty.
☐ may ☐ will not be entitled to a refund of part of the finance charge.

ASSUMPTION: Someone buying your property
☐ may ☐ may, subject to conditions ☐ may not assume the remainder of your loan on the original terms.

See your contract documents for any additional information about nonpayment, default, any required repayment in full before the scheduled date and prepayment refunds and penalties.

☐ * means an estimate ☐ all dates and numerical disclosures except the late payment disclosures are estimates.

* * NOTE: The Payments shown above include reserve deposits for Mortgage Insurance (if applicable), but exclude Property Taxes and Insurance.

THE UNDERSIGNED ACKNOWLEDGES RECEIVING A COMPLETED COPY OF THIS DISCLOSURE.

_____ (Applicant) _____ (Date)

_____ (Applicant) _____ (Date)

_____ (Applicant) _____ (Date)

_____ (Applicant) _____ (Date)

_____ (Lender) _____ (Date)

Calyx Form - lil isp (02/95)

Authorization to Check Credit

WAIVER OF PRIVACY — CREDIT CHECK AUTHORIZATION

Agency: _____   Phone: _____

Client's name: _____   Phone: _____

I authorize _____ to request a credit report and to act on my behalf as a third-party negotiator with lenders, landlords, or other appropriate entity in an effort to resolve current or possible future problems. All information pertaining to my case will be kept confidential and shall not be disclosed to any entity without my authorization. I understand that funding sources may review the information contained in the file, as a random review process.

MORTGAGE APPLICANTS: THIS FORM MUST BE SUBMITTED
TO LENDER AT TIME OF APPLICATION.

Counselor's Signature: _____   Phone: _____

Applicant's Signature: _____   Phone: _____

Address: _____

Co-applicant's Signature: _____   Phone: _____

Address: _____

Purchase Address: _____

Counseled or Referred (circle one).

Eligible for OHCD settlement grant?   Yes: ____   No: ____

❑ Counseled: Client completed counseling, including, but not limited to, fair housing law, employment evaluation, credit review, budget and is:

   ❑ Referred & Recommended: Client will be mortgage ready within 90 days.

   ❑ Referred & Not Recommended: Client is not ready for mortgage; additional counseling is needed.

   ❑ Post-Purchase: Client received counseling, which included, but is not limited to: housing care and management, availability to grants and loans, Predatory Lending practice, and referrals as needed.

Default & Delinquency: Client received counseling, which included, but is not limited to: communication with the lender to avoid foreclosure, assessment of future financial status, referrals to mortgage assistance programs such as HEMAP, FEMA, and HUD's Loss Mitigation, for which the client may be eligible.

Employment Verification

_____

Date: _____

To whom it may concern:

_____ has applied for residency (or is a resident) at one of [AGENCY/HOUSING COUNSELING ORGANIZATION] Units. As part of our processing, it is necessary that we obtain verification of his/her employment and anticipated gross annual Income. The applicant/resident hereby authorizes the release of information regarding his/her employment and income.

Please complete the section below and return it in the enclosed self-addressed envelope. (Please mail rather than have the above individual hand-deliver it.) Thank you in advance for your prompt attention.

Signature of Applicant/Resident _____

Signature of Property Manager _____

The Following to Be Completed by Employer

Pay Period (circle one):   weekly, biweekly, or monthly

Employed since: _____

Occupation: _____

Number of hours per week: _____

Hourly rate: _____

Overtime average per pay period: _____

Tips or commissions per pay period: _____

Type of employment (circle one):   full time, part time, temporary, or seasonal

Employer completing form: _____   Title: _____

Employer's signature: _____   Date: _____

If you have any questions please feel free to contact [HOUSING COUNSELOR/AGENT] at [PHONE NUMBER OF COUNSELOR/AGENT].

Mortgage Loan Comparison Worksheet

	LENDER 1	LENDER 2	LENDER 3
Name of lender			
Name of loan officer			
Phone number			
Date			
Basic information on the loan			
Loan program			
Loan amount requested			
Type of mortgage (fixed-rate, adjustable-rate, or other)			
Minimum down payment required			
Loan term			
Interest rate			
Annual percentage rate			
Points			
Monthly mortgage insurance premiums			
(PMI or MIP)			
How long MI must be kept			
Estimated monthly escrow for taxes and hazard insurance			
Ratios			
Estimated monthly payment (PITI, MI)			
Fees (different lenders have different names for fees and may charge different fees)			
Application fee			
Origination fee			
Processing fee			
Underwriting fee			

	LENDER 1	LENDER 2	LENDER 3
Appraisal fee			
Credit report fee			
Document preparation fee			
Broker fees			
Other fees			
Other loan considerations			
Prepayment penalties			
Is there a prepayment penalty?			
How much is the penaty?			
Rate lock-in			
Is the rate lock-in in writing?			
Is there a fee?			
When does lock-in occur?			
How long will the lock-in last?			
Adjustable-rate loan considerations			
What is the initial rate?			
How long does the initial rate last?			
How frequently does the rate change after the initial period?			
What are the rate caps for the first adjustment, each adjustment after that, and over the life of the loan?			
What index will be used?			
What is the margin?			
What is the highest possible monthly payment?			
Can the loan be converted to a fixed-rate one?			
Cost of conversion option			

Seller's Property Disclosure Statement

Property Address:

Seller:

A seller must disclose to a buyer all known material defects about property being sold that are not readily observable. This disclosure statement is designed to assist Seller in complying with disclosure requirements and to assist Buyer in evaluating the property being considered.

This Statement discloses Seller's knowledge of the condition of the property as of the date signed by Seller and is not a substitute for any inspections or warranties that Buyer may wish to obtain. This Statement is not a warranty of any kind by Seller or a warranty or representation by any listing real estate broker, any selling real estate broker, or their licensees. Buyer is encouraged to address concerns about the conditions of the property that may not be included in this Statement. This Statement does not relieve Seller of the obligation to disclose a material defect that may not be addressed on this form. A material defect is a problem with the property or any portion of it that would have a significant adverse impact on the value of the residential real property or that involves an unreasonable risk to people on the land.

1. **SELLER'S EXPERTISE**. Seller does not possess expertise in contracting, engineering, architecture, or other areas related to the construction and conditions of the property and its improvements, except as follows: _____

2. **OCCUPANCY**
   (a) Do you, Seller, currently occupy this property? ☐ Yes ☐ No
   If "no," when did you last occupy the property? _____
   (b) Have there been any pets living in the house or other structures during your ownership? ☐ Yes ☐ No
   If "yes," describe: _____

3. **ROOF**
   (a) Date roof installed: _____ Documented? ☐ Yes ☐ No ☐ Unknown
   (b) Has the roof been replaced or repaired during your ownership? ☐ Yes ☐ No
   If "yes," were the existing shingles removed? ☐ Yes ☐ No ☐ Unknown
   (c) Has the roof ever leaked during your ownership? ☐ Yes ☐ No
   (d) Do you know of any problems with the roof, gutters or downspouts? ☐ Yes ☐ No
   Explain any "yes" answers that you give in this section: _____

4. **BASEMENTS AND CRAWL SPACES (Complete only if applicable)**
   (a) Does the property have a sump pump? ☐ Yes ☐ No ☐ Unknown
   (b) Are you aware of any water leakage, accumulation, or dampness within the basement or crawl space? ☐ Yes ☐ No
   If "yes," describe in detail: _____
   (c) Do you know of any repairs or other attempts to control any water or dampness problem in the basement or crawl space? ☐ Yes ☐ No
   If "yes," describe the location, extent, date, and name of the person who did the repair or control effort: _____

5. TERMITES/WOOD-DESTROYING INSECTS, DRYROT, PESTS

(a) Are you aware of any termites/wood-destroying insects, dryrot, or pests affecting the property? ☐ Yes ☐ No

(b) Are you aware of any damage to the property caused by termites/wood-destroying insects, dryrot, or pests? ☐ Yes ☐ No

(c) Is your property currently under contract by a licensed pest control company? ☐ Yes ☐ No

(d) Are you aware of any termite/pest control reports or treatments for the property in the last five years? ☐ Yes ☐ No
Explain any "yes" answers that you give in this section, including the name of any service/treatment provider, if applicable:

6. STRUCTURAL ITEMS

(a) ☐ Yes ☐ No

(b) Are you aware of any past or present movement, shifting, deterioration, or other problems with walls, foundations, or other structural components? ☐ Yes ☐ No

(c) Are you aware of any past or present problems with driveways, walkways, patios, or retaining walls on the property? ☐ Yes ☐ No

(d) Is your property constructed with an Exterior Insulating Finishing System (EIFS), such as drivit or synthetic stucco? ☐ Yes ☐ No ☐ Unknown
If "yes," describe any known problems:

(e) Are there any defects in flooring, including stains? ☐ Yes ☐ No ☐ Unknown
If "yes," explain:
Explain any "yes" answers that you give in this section. When explaining efforts to control or repair, please describe the location and extent of the problem, and the date and person by whom the work was done, if known:

7. ADDITIONS/REMODELS
Have you made any additions, structural changes, or other alterations to the property? ☐ Yes ☐ No
If "yes," describe:

8. WATER AND SEWAGE

(a) What is the source of your drinking water? ☐ Public Water ☐ On-Site Water (Well on Property)
☐ Community Water ☐ None ☐ Other (explain):

(b) If your drinking water source is not public:
When was your water last tested? _____ What was the result of the test? _____
Is the pumping system in working order? ☐ Yes ☐ No
If "no," explain:

(c) Do you have a softener, filter, or other purification system? ☐ Yes ☐ No
If "yes," is the system ☐ Leased ☐ Owned

128. SELLER'S PROPERTY DISCLOSURE STATEMENT, 6/01   COPYRIGHT PENNSYLVANIA ASSOCIATION OF REALTORS® 1997
Version 6.09(5.5). ReaIFAST® Software Publishing Inc., (c) 2001 Reg# LPAPAR22354B, H. Daniel Caparo, Coldwell Banker

11/07/01 14:12:19

Page 1 of 4
Seller(s)

Seller's Property Disclosure Statement (continued)

(d) **What is the type of sewage system?** ☐ Public Sewer ☐ Individual On-lot Sewage Disposal System
☐ Individual On-lot Sewage Disposal System in Proximity to Well ☐ Community Sewage Disposal System
☐ Ten-acre Permit Exemption ☐ Holding Tank ☐ None ☐ None Available/Permit Limitations in Effect
☐ Other _____

If Individual On-lot, what type? ☐ Cesspool ☐ Drainfield ☐ Unknown ☐ Other (specify): _____
Is there a septic tank on the Property? ☐ Yes ☐ No ☐ Unknown
If "yes," what is the type of tank? ☐ Metal/steel ☐ Cement/concrete ☐ Fiberglass ☐ Unknown
☐ Other (specify): _____

Other type of sewage system (explain): _____

(e) **When was the on-site sewage disposal system last serviced?** _____
(f) **Is there a sewage pump?** ☐ Yes ☐ No
If "yes," is it in working order? ☐ Yes ☐ No
(g) **Is either the water or sewage system shared?** ☐ Yes ☐ No
If "yes," explain: _____

(h) **Are you aware of any leaks, backups, or other problems relating to any of the plumbing, water, and sewage-related items?**
☐ Yes ☐ No
If "yes," explain: _____

9. **PLUMBING SYSTEM**
(a) Type of plumbing: ☐ Copper ☐ Galvanized ☐ Lead ☐ PVC ☐ Unknown
☐ Other (explain): _____

(b) Are you aware of any problems with any of your plumbing fixtures (e.g., including but not limited to: kitchen, laundry, or bathroom fixtures; wet bars;
hot water heater; etc.)? ☐ Yes ☐ No
If "yes," explain: _____

10. **HEATING AND AIR CONDITIONING**
(a) Type of air conditioning: ☐ Central Electric ☐ Central Gas ☐ Wall ☐ None
Number of window units included in sale _____ Location _____
(b) List any areas of the house that are not air conditioned: _____

(c) Type of heating: ☐ Electric ☐ Fuel Oil ☐ Natural Gas ☐ Propane (On-site)
Are there wood or coal burning stoves? ☐ Yes ☐ No If "yes," how many? _____ Are they working? ☐ Yes ☐ No
Are there any fireplaces? ☐ Yes ☐ No If "yes," how many? _____ Are they working? ☐ Yes ☐ No
Other types of heating systems (explain): _____

(d) Are there any chimneys? ☐ Yes ☐ No If "yes," how many? _____ Are they working? ☐ Yes ☐ No
When were they last cleaned? _____

(e) List any areas of the house that are not heated:

(f) Type of water heating: ☐ Electric ☐ Gas ☐ Solar ☐ Other:

(g) Are you aware of any underground fuel tanks on the property? ☐ Yes ☐ No
If "yes," describe:

If tanks are not owned, explain:

(h) Are you aware of any problems with any item in this section? ☐ Yes ☐ No
If "yes," explain:

11. ELECTRICAL SYSTEM   Are you aware of any problems or repairs needed in the electrical system? ☐ Yes ☐ No
If "yes," explain:

12. OTHER EQUIPMENT AND APPLIANCES INCLUDED IN SALE (Complete only if applicable)
Equipment and appliances ultimately included in the sale will be determined by negotiation and according to the terms of the Agreement of Sale.

(a) ☐ Electric Garage Door Opener   No. of Transmitters
(b) ☐ Smoke Detectors   How many? _____ Location
(c) ☐ Security Alarm System   ☐ Owned ☐ Leased   Lease Information

(d) ☐ Lawn Sprinkler   No. _____   ☐ Automatic Timer
(e) ☐ Swimming Pool   ☐ Pool Heater   ☐ Spa/HotTub
     Pool/Spa Equipment (list):

(f) ☐ Refrigerator   ☐ Range   ☐ Microwave Oven   ☐ Dishwasher   ☐ Trash Compactor   ☐ Garbage Disposal
(g) ☐ Washer   ☐ Dryer
(h) ☐ Intercom
(i) ☐ Ceiling fans   No. _____   Location
(j) ☐ Other:

Are any items in this section in need of repair or replacement? ☐ Yes ☐ No ☐ Unknown
If "yes," explain:

13. LAND (SOILS, DRAINAGE, AND BOUNDARIES)
(a) Are you aware of any fill or expansive soil on the property? ☐ Yes ☐ No
(b) Are you aware of any sliding, setting, earth movement, upheaval, subsidence, or earth stability problems that have occurred on or affect the
property? ☐ Yes ☐ No

12B, SELLER'S PROPERTY DISCLOSURE STATEMENT, 6/01   COPYRIGHT PENNSYLVANIA ASSOCIATION OF REALTORS® 1997
Version 6.09(5.5). RealFAST® Software Publishing Inc., (c) 2001 Reg# LPAPAR22354B. H. Daniel Caparo, Coldwell Banker

Seller's Property Disclosure Statement (continued)

Note to Buyer: The property may be subject to mine subsidence damage. Maps of the counties and mines where mine subsidence damage may occur and mine subsidence insurance are available through:

Washington Road, McMurray, PA 15317 (800) 922-1678 (within Pennsylvania) or (724) 941-7100 (outside Pennsylvania).

(c) Are you aware of any existing or proposed mining, strip-mining, or any other excavations that might affect this property? ☐ Yes ☐ No

(d) To your knowledge, is this property, or part of it, located in a flood zone or wetlands area? ☐ Yes ☐ No

(e) Do you know of any past or present drainage or flooding problems affecting the property? ☐ Yes ☐ No

(f) Do you know of any encroachments, boundary line disputes, or easements? ☐ Yes ☐ No

Note to Buyer: Most properties have easements running across them for utility services and other reasons. In many cases, the easements do not restrict the ordinary use of the property, and Seller may not be readily aware of them. Buyers may wish to determine the existence of easements and restrictions by examining the property and ordering an Abstract of Title or searching the records in the Office of the Recorder of Deeds for the county before entering into an Agreement of Sale.

(g) Are you aware of any shared or common areas (e.g., driveways, bridges, docks, walls, etc.) or maintenance agreements? ☐ Yes ☐ No
Explain any "yes" answers that you give in this section:

14. HAZARDOUS SUBSTANCES

(a) Are you aware of any underground tanks (other than fuel tanks) or hazardous substances present on the property (structure or soil) such as, but not limited to, asbestos, Polychlorinated biphenyls (PCBs), Urea Formaldehyde Foam Insulation (UFFI), etc.? ☐ Yes ☐ No

(b) To your knowledge, has the property been tested for any hazardous substances? ☐ Yes ☐ No

(c) Explain any "yes" answers that you give in this section:

(d) Do you know of any tests for radon gas that have been performed in any buildings on the Property? ☐ Yes ☐ No
If "yes," list date, type, and results of all tests below:

DATE	TYPE OF TEST	RESULTS (picocuries/liter or working levels)	NAME OF TESTING SERVICE

(e) Are you aware of any radon removal system on the Property? ☐ Yes ☐ No
If "yes," list date installed and type of system, and whether it is in working order below:

DATE INSTALLED	TYPE OF SYSTEM	PROVIDER	WORKING ORDER
			☐ Yes ☐ No
			☐ Yes ☐ No
			☐ Yes ☐ No

(f) If Property was constructed, or if construction began, before 1978, you must disclose any knowledge of lead-based paint on the property. Are you aware of any lead-based paint or lead-based paint hazards on the property? ☐ Yes ☐ No
If "yes," explain how you know of it, where it is, and the condition of those lead-based paint surfaces:

(g) If Property was constructed, or if construction began, before 1978, you must disclose any reports or records of lead-based paint on the Property. Are you aware of any reports or records regarding lead-based paint or lead-based paint hazards on the Property? ☐ Yes ☐ No
If "yes," list all available reports and records:

15. CONDOMINIUMS AND OTHER HOMEOWNER ASSOCIATIONS (Complete only if applicable)
Type: ☐ Condominium ☐ Cooperative ☐ Homeowner Association or Planned Community ☐ Other

Notice Regarding Condominiums, Cooperatives, and Planned Communities: According to Section 3407 of the Uniform Condominium Act [68 Pa. C.S. §3407 (relating to resale of units) and 68 Pa. C.S. §3409 (relating to resale of cooperative interests)] and Section 5407 of the Uniform Planned Community Act [68 Pa. C.S. §5407 (relating to resale of units)], a buyer of a resale unit in a condominium, cooperative, or planned community must receive a copy of the declaration (other than the plats and plans), the by-laws, the rules or regulations, and a certificate of resale issued by the association in the condominium, cooperative, or planned community. The buyer will have the option of cancelling the agreement with the return of all deposit monies until the certificate has been provided to the buyer and for five days thereafter or until conveyance, whichever occurs first.

16. MISCELLANEOUS

(a) Are you aware of any historic preservation restriction or ordinance or archeological designation associated with the property? ☐ Yes ☐ No

(b) Are you aware of any existing or threatened legal action affecting the property? ☐ Yes ☐ No

(c) Do you know of any violations of federal, state, or local laws or regulations relating to this property? ☐ Yes ☐ No

(d) Are you aware of any public improvement, condominium or homeowner association assessments against the property that remain unpaid or of any violations of zoning, housing, building, safety or fire ordinances that remain uncorrected? ☐ Yes ☐ No

(e) Are you aware of any judgment, encumbrance, lien (for example co-maker or equity loan), overdue payment on a support obligation, or other debt against this property that cannot be satisfied by the proceeds of this sale? ☐ Yes ☐ No

(f) Are you aware of any reason, including a defect in title, that would prevent you from giving a warranty deed or conveying title to the property? ☐ Yes ☐ No

(g) Are you aware of any material defects to the property, dwelling, or fixtures which are not disclosed elsewhere on this form? ☐ Yes ☐ No
A material defect is a problem with the property or any portion of it that would have a significant adverse impact on the value of the residential real property or that involves an unreasonable risk to people on the land.
Explain any "yes" answers that you give in this section: _____

The undersigned Seller represents that the information set forth in this disclosure statement is accurate and complete to the best of Seller's knowledge. Seller hereby authorizes the Listing Broker to provide this information to prospective buyers of the property and to other real estate licensees. **SELLER ALONE IS RESPONSIBLE FOR THE ACCURACY OF THE INFORMATION CONTAINED IN THIS STATEMENT.** Seller shall cause Buyer to be notified in writing of any information supplied on this form which is rendered inaccurate by a change in the condition of the property following completion of this form.

EXECUTOR, ADMINISTRATOR, TRUSTEE SIGNATURE BLOCK

According to the provisions of the "Real Estate Seller Disclosure Act," the undersigned executor, administrator or trustee is not required to fill out a Seller's Property Disclosure Statement. The executor, administrator or trustee, must, however, disclose any known material defect(s) of the property.

_____ DATE _____

RECEIPT AND ACKNOWLEDGEMENT BY BUYER

The undersigned Buyer acknowledges receipt of this Disclosure Statement. Buyer acknowledges that this Statement is not a warranty and that, unless stated otherwise in the sales contract, Buyer is purchasing this property in its present condition. It is Buyer's responsibility to satisfy himself or herself as to the condition of the property. Buyer may request that the property be inspected, at Buyer's expense and by qualified professionals, to determine the condition of the structure or its components.

128. SELLER'S PROPERTY DISCLOSURE STATEMENT 8/01   COPYRIGHT PENNSYLVANIA ASSOCIATION OF REALTORS® 1997
Version 8.01(5.5); RealFAST® Software Publishing Inc. (c) 2001 Reg# LPAPAR223546, H. Daniel Caparo, Coldwell Banker

Settlement Statement (HUD-1)

A. Settlement Statement

U.S. Department of Housing and Urban Development

OMB Approval No. 2502-0265
(expires 9/30/2006)

B. Type of Loan

1. ☐ FHA   2. ☐ FmHA   3. ☐ Conv. Unins.
4. ☐ VA   5. ☐ Conv. Ins.

6. File Number: 7. Loan Number: 8. Mortgage Insurance Case Number:

C. Note: This form is furnished to give you a statement of actual settlement costs. Amounts paid to and by the settlement agent are shown. Items marked "(p.o.c.)" were paid outside the closing; they are shown here for informational purposes and are not included in the totals.

D. Name & Address of Borrower: E. Name & Address of Seller: F. Name & Address of Lender:

G. Property Location:

H. Settlement Agent:

Place of Settlement: I. Settlement Date:

J. Summary of Borrower's Transaction		K. Summary of Seller's Transaction	
100. Gross Amount Due From Borrower		400. Gross Amount Due To Seller	
101. Contract sales price		401. Contract sales price	
102. Personal property		402. Personal property	
103. Settlement charges to borrower (line 1400)		403.	
104.		404.	
105.		405.	
Adjustments for items paid by seller in advance		Adjustments for items paid by seller in advance	
106. City/town taxes	to	406. City/town taxes	to
107. County taxes	to	407. County taxes	to
108. Assessments	to	408. Assessments	to
109.		409.	
110.		410.	
111.		411.	
112.		412.	
120. Gross Amount Due From Borrower		420. Gross Amount Due To Seller	
200. Amounts Paid By Or In Behalf Of Borrower		500. Reductions In Amount Due To Seller	
201. Deposit or earnest money		501. Excess deposit (see instructions)	

202. Principal amount of new loan(s)	502. Settlement charges to seller (line 1400)
203. Existing loan(s) taken subject to	503. Existing loan(s) taken subject to
204.	504. Payoff of first mortgage loan
205.	505. Payoff of second mortgage loan
206.	506.
207.	507.
208.	508.
209.	509.

Adjustments for items unpaid by seller

		Adjustments for items unpaid by seller	
210. City/town taxes	to	510. City/town taxes	to
211. County taxes	to	511. County taxes	to
212. Assessments	to	512. Assessments	to
213.		513.	
214.		514.	
215.		515.	
216.		516.	
217.		517.	
218.		518.	
219.		519.	

220. Total Paid By/For Borrower	520. Total Reduction Amount Due Seller
300. Cash At Settlement From/To Borrower	**600. Cash At Settlement To/From Seller**
301. Gross Amount due from borrower (line 120)	601. Gross amount due to seller (line 420)
302. Less amounts paid by/for borrower (line 220)	602. Less reductions in amt. due seller (line 520)
303. Cash ☐ From ☐ To Borrower	603. Cash ☐ To ☐ From Seller

Section 5 of the Real Estate Settlement Procedures Act (RESPA) requires the following: • HUD must develop a Special Information Booklet to help persons borrowing money to finance the purchase of residential real estate to better understand the nature and costs of real estate settlement services; • Each lender must provide the booklet to all applicants from whom it receives or for whom it prepares a written application to borrow money to finance the purchase of residential real estate. • Lenders must prepare and distribute with the Booklet a Good Faith Estimate of the settlement costs that the borrower is likely to incur in connection with the settlement. These disclosures are mandatory.

Section 4(a) of RESPA mandates that HUD develop and prescribe this standard form to be used at the time of loan settlement to provide full disclosure of all charges imposed upon the borrower and seller. These are third party disclosures that are designed to provide the borrower with pertinent information during the settlement process in order to be a better shopper.

The Public Reporting Burden for this collection of information is estimated to average one hour per response, including the time for reviewing instructions, searching existing data sources, gathering and maintaining the data needed, and completing and reviewing the collection of information.

This agency may not collect this information, and you are not required to complete this form, unless it displays a currently valid OMB control number.

The information requested does not lend itself to confidentiality.

Previous editions are obsolete

Page 1 of 2

form HUD-1 (3/86)
ref Handbook 4305.2

Settlement Statement (HUD-1) (continued)

L. Settlement Charges	@	% =	Paid From Borrower's Funds at Settlement	Paid From Seller's Funds at Settlement
700. Total Sales/Broker's Commission based on price $				
Division of Commission (line 700) as follows:				
701. $	to			
702. $	to			
703. Commission paid at Settlement				
704.				
800. Items Payable In Connection With Loan				
801. Loan Origination Fee	%			
802. Loan Discount	%			
803. Appraisal Fee	to			
804. Credit Report	to			
805. Lender's Inspection Fee				
806. Mortgage Insurance Application Fee to				
807. Assumption Fee				
808.				
809.				
810.				
811.				
900. Items Required By Lender To Be Paid in Advance				
901. Interest from	to	@$	/day	
902. Mortgage Insurance Premium for		months to		
903. Hazard Insurance Premium for		years to		
904.		years to		
905.				
1000. Reserves Deposited With Lender				
1001. Hazard insurance	months @$	per month		
1002. Mortgage insurance	months @$	per month		
1003. City property taxes	months @$	per month		
1004. County property taxes	months @$	per month		
1005. Annual assessments	months @$	per month		
1006.	months @$	per month		
1007.	months @$	per month		
1008.	months @$	per month		
1100. Title Charges				
1101. Settlement or closing fee	to			
1102. Abstract or title search	to			
1103. Title examination	to			
1104. Title insurance binder	to			
1105. Document preparation	to			

1106. Notary fees   to
1107. Attorney's fees   to
      (includes above items numbers:
1108. Title insurance   to
      (includes above items numbers:
1109. Lender's coverage $
1110. Owner's coverage $
1111.
1112.
1113.

1200. Government Recording and Transfer Charges
1201. Recording fees: Deed $; Mortgage $; Releases $
1202. City/county tax/stamps: Deed $; Mortgage $
1203. State tax/stamps: Deed $; Mortgage $
1204.
1205.

1300. Additional Settlement Charges
1301. Survey   to
1302. Pest inspection to
1303.
1304.
1305.

1400. Total Settlement Charges (enter on lines 103, Section J and 502, Section K)

Previous editions are obsolete   Page 2 of 2   form HUD-1 (3/86)
                                                                        ref Handbook 4305.2

Mortgage Payment Invoice with Escrow

Nueva Esperanza Inc. Mortgage Company
1234 Main Street
Anytown, USA

[HOME OWNER/BORROWER]
1234 Anytown Street
Anytown, USA

ESCROW ACCOUNT DISCLOSURE STATEMENT This is an Estimate of Activity in Your Escrow Account During the Coming Year Based on Payments Anticipated to Be Made from Your Account.

This is an estimate and may change in the future. You will be notified if these amounts change.

MONTH	PAYMENTS TO ESCROW ACCOUNT	PAYMENTS FROM ESCROW ACCOUNT	DESCRIPTION	ESCROW ACCOUNT BALANCE
Initial Deposit				1,102.50
April	272.25	447.00	Insurance 927.75	
May	272.25	1,200.00		
June	272.25	1,472.25		
July	272.25	1,200.00	Property tax 544.50	
August	272.25	816.75		
September	272.25	1,089.00		
October	272.25	1,361.25		
November	272.25	1,633.50		
December	272.25	1,905.75		
January	272.25	1,620.00	Property Tax 000.00 School Tax 558.00	
February	272.25	830.25		
March	272.25	1,102.50		

(Please Keep This Statement for Comparison with Actual Activity in Your Account at the End of the Escrow Accounting Year.)

Cushion selected by servicer $544.50
Number of months for cushion: 2

[Your Monthly Mortgage Payment for the Coming Year will Be $1,250.00, of which $977.75 Will Be for Principal and Interest, $272.25 Will Go into Your Escrow Account, and $ Will Be for Discretionary Items (such as Life Insurance or Disability Insurance) that You Chose to Be Included with Your Monthly Payment.

The Terms of Your Loan May Result in Changes to the Monthly Principal and Interest Payments during the Year.]

Borrower [HOMEOWNER]
2007

- -

Please return this portion with your payment.

FROM: [HOMEOWNER/BORROWER]
        1234 Anytown Street
        Anytown, USA

Invoice # 100
Date: _____

        References
File No. XXXX
Loan # xxxx-xxxx
Amount Due: $1,250.00

TO: Nueva Esperanza Inc.
      Mortgage Company
      1234 Main Street
      Anytown, USA

Amount Enclosed:
$

9

The Language of Home Buying

The following are definitions of words used in the home-buying business. As in all languages, some words have dual meaning or overlapping meanings. While we cannot cover the entire gamut of the home-buying vocabulary, we have tried to define the more commonly used words. A copy of these pages is available for downloading at www.esperanza.us.

Abandonment Relinquishing all rights to a property.

Abstract of title A summary of the public records relating to the title of a property. A title insurance company or a lawyer reviews the abstract to determine if there are any problems that must be cleared up before the buyer can purchase. The title must be clear, marketable, and insurable.

Acceleration clause A provision in the mortgage that gives the lender the right to demand payment of the entire mortgage if a monthly payment is missed.

Acquired property A property that is acquired by foreclosure (or in place of foreclosure) or as the result of a paid insurance claim. Acquired property is also called *real estate owned* (REO).

Adjustable-rate mortgage (ARM) A mortgage loan whose interest rate changes (is adjusted) when general interest rates change. The rate is adjusted at specified times based on a national economic index and the lender's margin. When the rates change, the monthly payments are increased or reduced at times determined by the lender. There is usually a cap (limit) on the change to the rate of interest.

Amenity A feature of a home or property that is a benefit to the buyer but not a necessity. An amenity can be manmade (a pool, garage, or garden) or natural (location near a lake or park).

Amortization The process of paying off a loan with regular payments over a fixed period of time. An *amortization schedule* is the timetable for payment for the period of the loan (for example, fifteen or thirty years); it shows the amount of principal and interest that each payment covers, and the balance remaining until you own the home.

Annual mortgage statement Each year, the owner should receive a report on the mortgage; it will give details of the taxes and interest paid and the remaining balance of the principal.

Annual percentage rate (APR) The cost of borrowing money. The cost is presented as yearly interest rate and includes all the expenses associated with the loan: interest, points, mortgage insurance, and other fees.

Application The first step in the official loan-approval process. The *application form* contains information about the person applying to borrow money. The *application fee* is a one-time charge by the lender to cover the costs of processing the application for a mortgage loan; the fee may include the cost of a credit report and appraisal of the property.

Appraisal A professional opinion of the market value of the property. The document containing the opinion is also called an appraisal. The lender usually requires an appraisal to make sure that the mortgage loan amount is not greater than the value of the property. The *appraiser* is a qualified professional who conducts the appraisal, makes the estimate of value, and prepares the appraisal document.

Appreciation An increase in value. The value of a home may increase because of changes in market conditions, improvements that the owner makes, or other factors.

Approved lender A financial institution approved by a loan insurer.

Arrears Debts, debt payments, or bills, such as rent, that are overdue are in arrears.

Assessed value. The value placed on the house; this value determines the amount of property taxes that are *assessed*. An *assessor* is a government official who determines the value of a property for tax purposes.

Asset Anything that you own that can be sold or exchanged; anything with commercial value.

Assumable mortgage A mortgage that can be transferred from a seller to a buyer. Once the buyer assumes the loan, the seller is no longer responsible for repaying it. The process of transfer from buyer to seller usually includes a fee and a credit package.

Attachment Legal seizure of a debtor's property or income to satisfy a financial obligation.

Authorized user account A credit agreement with a person with no legal responsibility for paying but who is authorized to make charges on the account with the account owner's permission.

Automated underwriting A computer-based method that mortgage lenders use to process and approve (or deny) loan applications quickly. It uses credit scores and other information about the borrower.

Balloon mortgage A loan with low payments of principal for an initial period of time (five, seven, or ten years); after that, the borrower must pay the entire balance of the loan or refinance it.

Bank An institution that offers financial services, such as checking and savings accounts, consumer loans, safe-deposit boxes, investments, and automatic bill payment. Banks must follow state and federal regulations.

Bankruptcy A process in which a person's assets are turned over to a trustee and sold to pay off outstanding debts. A person may file for bankruptcy when he or she owes more than he or she can repay, or he or she may be forced by creditors into involuntary bankruptcy.

Basis point One one-hundredth of 1 percent (0.01 percent).

Binder An offer that is secured by a deposit (sometimes called earnest money) or down payment.

Borrower A person who has been approved to receive a loan. The borrower is obligated to repay the loan and any related fees according to the terms of the loan.

Budget A detailed plan for coordinating resources and expenditures.

Building code A set of regulations for the design, construction, and materials of a building. A building code is based on safety standards. Codes differ from place to place.

Building line The fixed distance extending inward from the boundaries of the lot or property, beyond which the building cannot extend. The building line is established by deed restrictions, building codes, or zoning ordinances.

Buydown A sum of money paid to a lender at closing to reduce the borrower's monthly payments for a specific period of time.

Cancellation clause A clause in a contract that allows either party to terminate the contract under certain agreed conditions.

Cap A limit on how much an interest rate can be increased or reduced. A cap is placed on adjustable-rate mortgages (ARMs).

Capitalization The process of applying delinquent monthly payments to the outstanding principal balance of a mortgage.

Cash reserve A lender sometimes requires that a borrower have a certain amount of cash (usually the total of a specific number of monthly mortgage payments) available in reserve in addition to the down payment and closing costs.

Certificate of title A document provided by a qualified source (usually a title company) that shows that the property legally belongs to the current owner, who is therefore legally free to sell it. The certificate ensures a *clear title*. Before the title is transferred at closing, it must be free and clear of all liens and other claims.

Chattel A loan secured by personal property; this is common practice in financing manufactured homes.

Closing The time when the property is formally sold and transferred from the seller to the buyer. Closing (also called *settlement*) usually occurs at a meeting of the buyer, seller, settlement agent, and real estate agent. The buyer signs the mortgage and the mortgage note. The seller receives payment for the property. The buyer or seller (or both) pays the *closing costs*. The title is transferred from the seller to the buyer.

Closing costs The expenses, which vary by region, over and above the purchase price of the property; the lender must provide details of the closing costs when the borrower applies for the loan.

Collateral Property accepted as security for a loan. It is one of the four C's of buying power. The appraisal value must be equal to or greater than the sale price.

Collection account A delinquent account that has been transferred from the creditor to a professional debt-collection firm.

Commission An amount (usually a percentage of the purchase price) that the real estate professional collects for his or her part in negotiating the transaction.

Commitment A written agreement between a lender and a borrower stating that the lender will loan money to the borrower if the borrower complies with the stated conditions. When the applicant is approved to receive the loan, the lender provides a *commitment letter* stating those terms.

Community Reinvestment Act (CRA) A federal law that requires lenders to meet the credit needs of their local communities.

Comparative market analysis (CMA) A written analysis of comparable properties currently available for sale or sold in the last six months.

Conditional sales contract A contract for the sale of a property in which the transfer of title to the buyer is contingent on the fulfillment of certain conditions.

Contingency An event that must happen for the sale to take place. A condition that is part of the offer on a property.

Contract A legal agreement between two or more parties.

Contract for deed A type of financing offered by a seller: the buyer makes a down payment and pays the seller installment payments. The seller does not transfer the title until the loan is fully repaid or refinanced.

Contractor An individual hired to build, remodel, or repair a property. Contractors should be licensed in their particular trade and region and should have insurance and be bonded.

Conventional loan (conventional mortgage) A loan from the private sector that is not guaranteed or insured by the U.S. government.

Convertible mortgage An adjustable-rate mortgage (ARM) that can be converted to a fixed-rate mortgage under certain conditions.

Conveyance The transfer of a title on real property from one party to another.

Covenant A clause in a mortgage that obligates or restricts the borrower; violation of the covenant can result in foreclosure.

Credit bureau score Used to determine a person's ability to qualify for a loan, the credit bureau score is a number that attempts to indicate the likelihood that the borrower might not repay the loan (default). The credit bureau score is based on *credit history,* which is the record for the person's debt payment. The credit history appears on the person's *credit report,* a record that lists all past and present debts and repayments. A *credit derogative* on the credit report reflects slow paying, open collection accounts, liens, or judgments.

Debt A sum of money owed that must be paid by an expressed agreement.

Debt-to-income ratio The ratio of total debt payments to gross income (also called *back-end ratio).*

Deductible The amount by which an insurance company reduces the size of its payment for covered damage or loss.

Deed A legal document of the title (ownership) to a property (also called a *grant deed* or *warranty deed).*

Deed-in-lieu An agreement in which a delinquent borrower gives the lender the deed and the keys and moves out of the property in exchange for forgiveness of the loan (also called *deed-in-lieu foreclosure*).

Deed of trust An alternative in some states to a mortgage. A third party holds the deed to the property as security until the borrower repays the loan (also called a *trust deed*).

Default Failure to make loan payments when they are due. Failure to meet financial obligations may result in foreclosure on the loan (also called *delinquency*).

Deposit A cash payment made by a potential buyer to show that his or her offer is serious.

Depreciation A reduction in the value of the property over time due to changes in the market conditions, wear and tear, or other factors.

Disclosure The seller is required by federal or state law to provide information about the property for sale, especially defects and actual or potential problems.

Discounted payoff An agreement negotiated with a creditor that allows a borrower to pay less money than is actually owed to cease collection activities (also called *settlement*).

Discount point An amount paid at closing to reduce the interest rate on the loan. A point is usually 1 percent of the total amount of the loan.

Discretionary income The amount of money left over in a month after regular expenses are subtracted from the take-home pay.

Document recording The process of recording certain documents and making them part of the public record of the transaction and transfer of property.

Down payment The amount of cash a borrower provides; it is not part of the mortgage loan. The down payment is usually a given percentage of the total purchase price.

Dual agent A real estate agent who represents both the buyer and the seller in a transaction.

Due-on-sale clause A provision in a mortgage that allows the lender to demand repayment in full if the borrower sells the property.

Earnest money Money put down (a deposit) or a down payment by a potential buyer to show that he or she is serious about purchasing the property. If the seller accepts the offer, the earnest money becomes part of the down payment. If the seller declines the offer, he or she returns it. If the buyer pulls out of the deal, he or she forfeits the earnest money.

Employment verification (EV) A form sent to the borrower's employer to verify his or her employment and employment history.

Encroachment An obstruction, building, or part of a building that intrudes beyond a legal boundary onto neighboring private or public land or a building extending beyond the building line.

Encumbrance A legal right or interest in a property that affects a clear title and reduces the property's value. The encumbrance can be a lien, mortgage, zoning ordinance, or other claim. It does not legally prevent transfer. If a title search reveals an encumbrance, the buyer must decide whether to take the property and deal with the encumbrance.

Energy-efficient mortgage (EEM) A federal program in the FHA that helps home buyers save money on utility bills. As part of the purchase, home buyers can finance the cost of adding energy-efficient features to a new or existing home.

Equal Credit Opportunity Act (ECOA) A federal law that prohibits lenders from denying mortgages on the basis of race, color, religion, national origin, age, sex, or marital status.

Equity An owner's financial interest in the property; how much of the property the owner actually owns. To calculate equity, subtract the amount still owed on the mortgage from the fair market value of the property. The result is the owner's equity.

Escalator clause A clause in a mortgage that allows for a periodic increase in the interest rate under certain conditions.

Escrow account A separate account into which the lender puts a portion of each monthly mortgage payment. The lender uses this to pay property taxes, homeowner's insurance, and mortgage insurance.

Fair Credit Reporting Act A consumer protection law that regulates how consumer credit reports are disclosed.

Fair Housing Act A law that prohibits discrimination in all stages of the home-buying process on the basis of race, color, national origin, religion, age, sex, marital status, or disability.

Fair market value The hypothetical price that a willing buyer and seller would agree to if they acted freely, carefully, and with complete knowledge of the situation.

Fannie Mae The Federal National Mortgage Association (FNMA), a federally charted enterprise owned by private shareholders. Fannie Mae purchases residential mortgages and converts them into securities for sale to investors. By purchasing mortgages, Fannie Mae supplies funds to lenders so they can offer more loans.

Federal Home Loan Bank (FHLB) The Federal Home Loan Bank system was created in 1932 by the Federal Home Loan Bank Act to restore confidence in the nation's financial institutions and to increase the supply of funds to local lenders who in turn finance loans for home mortgages. Since 1989, the Federal Home Loan Bank System's public policy mission has been expanded to include Affordable Housing and Community Development lending.

Federal Housing Administration (FHA) Since 1934, the FHA has advanced home ownership for all Americans. FHA provides mortgage insurance to lenders to cover most losses from borrower defaults. This encourages lenders to make loans to borrowers who may not qualify for conventional mortgages.

First mortgage A loan that has priority over the claims of subsequent lenders on the same property if the borrower defaults.

Fixed expense An expense that does not change from period to period, such as loan payments or rent.

Fixed-rate mortgage A mortgage on which the payments remain the same over the life of the loan.

Flexible expense An expense that changes from month to month, such as groceries or personal items.

Flood insurance A policy required by the lender if the property is located on a flood plain.

Forbearance An agreement by the lender to allow a delinquent borrower to skip one or more payments and make them up later through a payment plan.

Foreclosure The legal process by which a mortgaged property is sold to pay the loan of a defaulting borrower.

For sale by owner A home that is offered for sale without the use of a real estate agent.

Freddie Mac The Federal Home Loan Mortgage Corporation (FHLMC) is a federally chartered corporation that purchases residential mortgages, converts them into securities, and sells them to investors. This provides lenders with funds to serve new home buyers.

Gift letter A document required by a lender if a borrower receives the funds for a down payment as a gift from another.

Ginnie Mae The Government National Mortgage Association (GNMA) is a government-owned corporation overseen by the U.S. Department of Housing and Urban Development. Ginnie Mae pools FHA-insured and VA-guaranteed loans to back securities for private investment. The income allows lenders to provide loans to new home buyers.

Good-faith estimate A document from the lender that lists the anticipated closing costs.

Graduated payment mortgage A loan that starts out with lower monthly payments, then gradually rises over a period of years, then remains fixed for the remainder of the loan period.

Gross income Money earned before taxes and other deductions.

Hazard insurance Insurance to protect the homeowner against the costs of physical damage to the property and its contents from wind, fire, theft, vandalism, and other perils. See *homeowner's insurance.*

Homebuyer Education Learning Program (HELP) An educational program offered by the FHA that counsels people about the home-buying process.

Home equity line of credit A type of loan that allows the homeowner to obtain money by check or a credit card; the collateral for the loan is the property.

Home equity loan A loan whose amount is limited to the difference between the amount of equity the homeowner has in the property and the home's market value.

Home inspection An examination of the structure and mechanical systems to check a home's safety and whether any repairs are needed. A home inspection is done by a *licensed home inspector.*

Homeowner's insurance An insurance policy that combines protection against damage to the property and its contents with protection against claims of negligence or inappropriate action that result in someone's injury or property damage.

Home warranty Offers protection for the mechanical systems and attached appliances (for example, the heating system and hot water heater) against unexpected repairs not covered by homeowner's insurance. The coverage is for a specific time and does not cover the structure of the home.

Housing counseling agency Provides counseling, classes, and assistance to individuals seeking to buy and own a home. A *certified housing counselor* can help a buyer through the entire process, from planning through ownership.

HUD The U.S. Department of Housing and Urban Development, a federal government entity. Since 1965, HUD has worked to create decent and suitable living environments for all Americans. HUD enforces fair housing laws and improves and develops communities.

HUD-1 Settlement Statement An itemized list of all closing costs. It must be given to the borrower at or before closing (also known as the *settlement sheet).*

HVAC Stands for heating, ventilation, and air conditioning; this is the home's heating and cooling system (a mechanical system).

Index A measurement that lenders use to determine changes to the interest rate charged on adjustable-rate mortgages (ARMs).

Inflation During periods of inflation, the number of dollars in circulation is greater than the amount of goods and services available for purchase. Inflation leads to lower buying power of the dollar.

Insurance Protection against a specific loss over a period of time; the protection is secured by a regularly scheduled payment, called a premium.

Interest A fee charged for borrowing money.

Interest factor The cost for borrowing each $1,000 of a mortgage loan, based on interest rate and term.

Interest rate The amount of interest charged on a monthly loan payment, usually expressed as an annual percentage.

Interest rate lock-in A written guarantee that the borrower will receive the loan at a specific interest rate if the closing is held within a specified time.

Joint account A credit agreement with two persons in which each is liable for payment. Also a savings or checking account with two people, each of whom may deposit or withdraw funds.

Joint tenancy A form of ownership in which two or more people have an equal and undivided interest in the property.

Judgment A legal decision. When a legal decision requires repayment of debt, it may include a property lien, which as collateral secures the creditor's claim. A judgment may be listed on a credit report.

Land lease An arrangement where the person owns the house but rents the land it is on.

Lease-purchase (or lease-purchase mortgage) A way to purchase a home, lease-purchase is often a way for low-income and moderate-income people to become homeowners. The person leases (rents) the property with the option to buy. The monthly rent includes an extra payment that is deposited into a savings account to be used as a down payment and for closing costs.

Lender The entity that offers a mortgage loan (also called a *mortgagee*).

Liability protection Insurance that covers the insured homeowner against injury to other people and damage to their personal property through his or her negligence.

Lien A legal hold or claim of one person or entity on the property of another as security for debt, a charge that may be listed on a credit report as public record. A lien must be satisfied when the property is sold.

Listing agent A real estate professional who has a contract with the seller of a house to advertise the property for sale and represent the seller when offers are made (also called a *seller's agent*).

Loan Money borrowed, usually to be repaid with interest.

Loan fees Costs associated with processing of a loan.

Loan fraud Purposely giving incorrect information on a loan application in order to qualify for a loan. Loan fraud may result in civil or criminal penalties.

Loan modification An agreement between a lender and a delinquent borrower to change the terms of the loan.

Loan term The amount of time a borrower has to pay off a loan.

Loan-to-value ratio (LTV) The ratio of the loan balance to the appraised value of the property. Calculate by dividing the amount borrowed by the appraised value of the property. The higher the LTV, the less cash a borrower must provide as down payment.

Lock-in A written agreement guaranteeing the buyer a specific interest rate if the loan is closed in a specified time. This is part of the loan commitment.

Loss mitigation A process to avoid foreclosure. The lender tries to help a borrower who has been unable to make loan payments and is therefore in danger of defaulting on the loan.

Margin A margin is a percentage amount set and disclosed by a lender. It is added to the current index rate to calculate an ARM rate on the mortgage's anniversary.

Mortgage A lien on the property that secures the promise to repay a loan.

Mortgage banker A company that originates loans and sells them to secondary mortgage lenders, such as Fannie Mae or Freddie Mac.

Mortgage broker A firm that originates and processes loans for many different lenders.

Mortgagee The lender.

Mortgage insurance A policy that protects lenders against some or most of the losses that can occur when a borrower defaults on a mortgage loan. Mortgage insurance is usually required for borrowers whose down payment is less than 20 percent of the purchase price. The borrower pays a *mortgage insurance premium (MIP)*; this monthly payment is usually part of the mortgage payment.

Mortgage modification A loss-mitigation option that allows a borrower to refinance or extend the term of the mortgage loan and thus reduce monthly payments.

Mortgagor The borrower.

Negative amortization Payment term under which the borrower's monthly payments do not cover the interest due, thereby increasing the loan balance.

Net income The borrower's income minus withheld federal income tax and other deductions.

Nontraditional credit history A record of credit performance shown by receipts and check stubs for payments to landlords, utility companies, and child-care providers. Nontraditional credit is useful for loan applicants who have no credit history from loans or other forms of credit.

Note A written promise by one party to pay a specified sum of money to a second party under mutually agreed-upon conditions (also called a *promissory note*).

Note rate The interest rate on a mortgage loan.

Offer A potential buyer's indication, usually in writing, that he or she is willing to buy a property at a specific price.

Open thirty-day account A credit agreement in which the borrower agrees to promise to repay each month the full balance owed.

Origination The process of preparing, submitting, and evaluating a loan application. Origination usually includes a credit check, verification of employment, and an appraisal of the property to be purchased. The *origination fee* is the charge for processing the loan; the fee is usually calculated as points (a percentage of the loan amount) and paid at closing.

Partial claim A loss-mitigation option offered by the FHA; it allows the borrower, with help from a lender, to get an interest-free loan from HUD to bring mortgage payments up to date.

Payment plan An agreement with a lender in which the borrower promises to make up for any missed payments by sending one full payment and one partial payment each month until the delinquent mortgage payments are up to date.

PITI Stands for principal, interest, taxes, and insurance. These are the four parts of a monthly mortgage payment.

Planned unit development (PUD) A type of property that is part of a subdivision and has common areas for the use of all residents that are maintained by fees paid to the homeowners association. Usually the owner of a PUD owns both the dwelling and the land it is on.

PMI Stands for private mortgage insurance. Privately owned companies offer standard and special affordable mortgage insurance for qualified borrowers.

Point A point is a fee equal to 1 percent of the loan amount.

Preapproval A guarantee that the lender will loan a potential borrower a fixed amount as long as the borrower buys a home within a certain period of time and the house is appraised for no more than the amount of money for which the borrower qualified.

Predatory lending A type of lending that falls between appropriate, risk-based pricing and blatant fraud.

Preforeclosure sale When a lender agrees to allow a delinquent borrower to sell the property to avoid foreclosure.

Premium An amount paid for insurance.

Prepayment Paying more each month than the amount of the mortgage loan payment so as to pay the loan off sooner and save money on interest charges.

Prepayment penalty On some loans a fee charged if the borrower pays the loan off before it is due.

Prequalification An informal process lenders use to calculate how large a mortgage they can lend a potential borrower. A prequalification is based on unverified information.

Prime lending Lending to borrowers with highly rated credit histories. Prime loans are usually called *A loans*.

Principal The amount borrowed from a lender. It does not include the interest and other fees.

Qualifying income ratios The ratio of proposed monthly housing expense to gross monthly income or total monthly debt payments, including proposed housing expense, to gross monthly income.

Radon A radioactive gas found in some homes that if in strong concentration can cause health problems.

Real estate agent An individual who works for a real estate broker and is licensed to negotiate and arrange real estate sales. In some states, a licensed person who acts on behalf of the buyer and is paid a commission by the seller.

Real Estate Settlement Procedures Act (RESPA) A federal law that protects consumers from abuse during the residential real estate purchase and loan process. This law requires all lenders to disclose all settlement costs, practices, and relationships.

Realtor A real estate agent or broker who is a member of the National Association of Realtors and its local and state associations.

Refinancing Paying off one loan by obtaining another. Refinancing is usually done to secure better terms, such as a lower interest rate or shorter loan period.

Rehabilitation mortgage A mortgage that covers the cost of rehabilitating (repairing or improving) a property. Some rehabilitation mortgages—for example, FHA's 203(k)—allow the borrower to combine the cost of rehabilitation and home purchase into one mortgage loan.

Revolving credit A credit agreement that allows borrowers to pay all or part of the outstanding balance on a loan or credit card. As credit is paid off, it becomes available again to use for another purchase or cash advance.

Risk-based pricing A system that assesses borrowing risks by loan to determine interest rates and fees for mortgage loans.

Secondary market Investors who purchase residential mortgages originated by primary lenders and thereby provide lenders with money for future lending.

Second mortgage A home loan whose lender has rights subordinate to the rights of the first mortgage. In foreclosure, this second mortgagee is repaid after the first mortgage.

Servicing The collection of payments and management of a mortgage.

Settlement Another term for closing.

Settlement statement A document required by RESPA. This is an itemized statement of the services and charges related to the closing or settlement of the property transfer (also called *HUD-1 Settlement Statement* or *Uniform Settlement Statement*).

Sole and separate A form of ownership in which one individual owns the property.

Special forbearance A loss-mitigation option. The lender arranges a revised repayment plan for the borrower; the plan may include a temporary reduction or suspension of monthly loan payments.

Specifications A detailed description of the size, shape, materials, and other details of a building or remodeling project.

Subprime lending A type of lending that relies on risk-based pricing. It serves borrowers who cannot obtain credit in the prime market, in which higher-risk borrowers pay high costs for loans. Subprime loans are often called *A-through-D* credits.

Survey A professional measurement of a property. A professional survey results in a diagram of the property that indicates legal boundaries, easements, encroachments, rights-of-way, improvement locations, and other aspects of the property.

Sweat equity Using one's labor to build or improve a property as part of the down payment.

Tenancy in common A form of ownership in which two or more people own a property and retain separate shares of ownership.

Title A legal document that establishes the ownership of a property.

Title insurance Insurance to protect the lender (lender's policy) or the buyer (owner's policy) against loss arising from disputes over ownership of a property.

Title I An FHA-insured loan that allows a borrower to make renovations or repairs (nonluxury improvements) to a home. Title I loans of less than $7,500 do not require a lien.

Title search A check of public records to confirm that the seller is a recognized owner of the property and that there are no unsettled liens or other claims against it.

Transfer tax State or local tax payable when the title is transferred from one owner to another.

Truth-in-lending A federal law that requires lenders to give full written disclosure of all fees, terms, and conditions associated with the loan.

Two-step mortgage A type of adjustable-rate mortgage that has one interest rate for a specific period of time and another for the rest of the loan period.

Underwriting The process of analyzing a loan application to determine the amount of risk in making the loan. Underwriting includes a review of the potential borrower's credit and an appraisal of the property.

VA The Department of Veterans Affairs is a federal agency that guarantees loans made to veterans. Similar to mortgage insurance, a loan guarantee protects the lender against loss from a borrower's defaulting.

Verification of deposit (VOD) A form sent to each depository listed on the loan application to verify that funds the owner claims to have are there.

Waive To give up a claim or right. A written agreement to give up a claim or right is a *waiver*.

Yield The effective rate of return on a mortgage, based on fees, the interest rate, and the price paid for it.

Bibliography

The Bible. Contemporary English Version. The American Bible Society.

Bipartisan Millennial Housing Commission, appointed by the Congress of the United States. *Meeting Our Nation's Housing Challenges.* Washington, D.C.: United States Congress, 2002.

Harkness, Joseph M., and Sandra J. Newman. "Effects of Homeownership on Children: The Role of Neighborhood Characteristics and Family Income." Federal Reserve Board of New York. *Economic Policy Review,* June 2003: 87–107.

Haurin, Donald R., Toby L. Parcel, and Jean R. Haurin. "The Impact of Homeownership on Child Outcomes." Joint Center for Housing Studies of Harvard University, October 2001.

Howe, Peter E. "Low-Income Homeownership Literature Review." Department of Economics, Maxwell School of Citizenship and Public Affairs, Syracuse University, November 10, 2003.

Rohe, William M., and Shannon and McCarthy Van Zandt. "The Social Benefits and Costs of Homeownership: A Critical Assessment of the Research." Joint Center for Housing Studies of Harvard University, October 2001: 1–31.

United States Housing and Urban Development. "Urban Policy Brief Number 2." August 1995.

Acknowledgments

There are many people who have assisted me in the writing of this book, and I very much appreciate the opportunity to acknowledge their support. First, to my family members, Dee, Sito, and Tata, who reviewed some of the text and made several helpful comments. Second, the administrative help of Arlene Larsen saved me much time and effort. The director of housing for Nueva Esperanza, Maritza Ortiz, took the time to review my notes and provide some missing pieces. My friends Nelson Acevedo, a board member of Nueva Esperanza and mortgage banker, and Nancy Perez, an insurance saleswoman, reviewed portions of the text and helped me explain the nuances of mortgage and insurance products, and the closing processes. I thank the board of directors of Nueva Esperanza and Hispanic Clergy for allowing me to proceed with this project.

At Simon & Schuster, my thanks go to copyeditor David Hawkins, to whom I owe a handshake; my editor, Johanna Castillo, who convinced me to forge ahead with the Esperanza Series and showed great trust and confidence in my work; and Judith Curr, publisher of Atria Books.

To those of you who have read this text, I pray a blessing in your search for a house that you will transform into a home. And as in all things, I am most grateful to Jesus Christ, who allows me breath to be able to fulfill my lifelong dream of publishing a book that will be of value to someone. To that end I say AMEN.

ATRIA BOOKS

For information on
how to place a bulk order
for this or any other
Simon & Schuster title,
please call

1-800-456-6798

ATRIA BOOKS
A Division of Simon & Schuster
A CBS COMPANY
www.simonsays.com